"If you feel like you're simultaneously 'too much' and 'not enough,' Carey gets you, gives you hope, perfect One, in whose love you ar

for the "Perfect

and Start Living Braver

"Every woman I know (including me) struggles with insecurity in some way. We need to be reminded of who we are in Christ and have strategies that help us apply this truth to our lives. That's exactly what Carey Scott offers in these pages—encouragement for your heart and practical tools for your mind that will help you truly get free from insecurity."

—**Holley Gerth**, *Wall Street Journal* bestselling author

"Carey Scott delves deep to identify the roots of a woman's insecurities; all the while, she infuses us with hope by revealing the Source of our healing. Carey's transparency is permission for women to gently unwrap our own areas of insecurity. Her faith leads us to change and freedom."

—**Amy Carroll**, Proverbs 31 Ministries speaker;
author of *Breaking Up with Perfect*

"In *Untangled*, Carey Scott helps us identify and discover how to be biblically set free from those things that hold our hearts captive and prevent us from living the abundant life Jesus died to give us. With vulnerable transparency, Carey shares her personal 'tangles' and gives readers the tools they need to overcome their own. If we want to fully embrace our God-given destinies, we must first become untangled— and Carey Scott helps us do just that. A definite must-read!

—**Stephanie Shott**, founder of the MOM Initiative;
author of *The Making of a Mom*

"Carey Scott is a fresh voice for women. Her straightforward, authentic approach to life and her willingness to share even the deepest parts of it combine beautifully with her love for the Lord. This book made me laugh and it made me cry, but most importantly it reminded me that even in the darkest times and places in life, my hope can be found in Christ."

—**Jill Hart**, founder of Christian Work at Home Ministries;
author of *Do Life Different*

"With unflinching transparency and vulnerability, Carey takes readers on a journey that leads to freedom. One by one, she loosens the ties that bind our value to our appearance, performance, and other people. And then she anchors it firmly to the only unchanging Source of worth we have: Jesus Christ. This is a must-read book for any woman who struggles with feelings of inadequacy—and isn't that every one of us?"

—**Melinda Means**, speaker; coauthor of *Mothering from Scratch: Finding the Best Parenting Style for You and Your Family*

"Carey Scott masterfully unravels each of the tangles we women can't help but find our way into. With her relatable voice and compassionate heart, she gently guides readers away from such struggles while loosening the knots we desperately want to break free from. A must-read!"

—**Jenny Lee Sulpizio**, author of *For the Love of God: A Woman's Guide to Finding Faith and Getting Grace* and *Confessions of a Wonder Woman Wannabe*

"The big question most women face in life is this: What makes us significant? Beyond that, we wonder if we are really worth loving. So many of us are content to trade admiration or approval for the love we need more than anything. In her brave book, Carey Scott rips back the curtain of her own private struggles and invites us to take a good hard look at this question in our own hearts: How many opportunities in life—how many chances at love—will we miss because of the tangled up mess of insecurity in our soul? I found myself thinking, *I didn't even realize that was still a struggle for me!* Carey reminds us in profound ways that life is too short, energy is too precious, and we are too valuable in God's eyes to be strangled by knots of insecurity. Allow Carey to take your hand and encourage you so that, starting today, you can begin (or begin again) the brave story of the rest of your life."

—**Laurie Wallin**, life coach; author of *Why Your Weirdness Is Wonderful: Embrace Your Quirks & Live Your Strengths*; LaurieWallin.com

Untangled

Let God Loosen
the Knots of Insecurity
in Your Life

Carey Scott

Revell

a division of Baker Publishing Group
Grand Rapids, Michigan

Published by Revell
a division of Baker Publishing Group
P.O. Box 6287, Grand Rapids, MI 49516-6287
www.revellbooks.com

Printed in the United States of America

Library of Congress Cataloging-in-Publication Data
Scott, Carey, 1966–
    Untangled : let God loosen the knots of insecurity in your life / Carey Scott.
    pages cm
    Includes bibliographical references.
    ISBN 978-0-8007-2659-1 (pbk.)
    1. Security (Psychology)—Religious aspects—Christianity. 2. Peace of mind—Religious aspects—Christianity. I. Title.
    BV4908.5.S385 2015
    248.4—dc23   2014047670

Published in association with Jessica Kirkland, with the literary agency The Blythe Daniel Agency.

15 16 17 18 19 20 21   7 6 5 4 3 2 1

This book is dedicated to my husband, Wayne—my cheerleader, my encourager, my constant. You gave me courage to walk this journey. You helped me trust again. You reminded me that I mattered. Thank you for seeing the real me through the tangles of my life. I love you.

Contents

Acknowledgments

I want to recognize my husband, Wayne, for being Mr. Amazing. There's no one else I'd rather navigate the waters of life with than you. We've been through so much and have come out even stronger. I absolutely adore you!

To my kids, Sam and Sara, no mom has ever been more proud. I love how we laugh, try to scare each other, do goofy things together, and have amazing conversations about life. You are my greatest contributions to the world. Thanks for loving me in my imperfection without making me feel as though I have any. You two rock my world.

Thanks to my mom, dad, and sister for loving me even when it was hard. And I know it was from time to time. You're a wonderful family, and I am grateful for all you've done for me.

To my agent, Jessie Kirkland, you're awesome. You believed in me way before I did. You patiently coached me as my writing style evolved from the King James Version to the Message. Thank you for giving me the courage to find my voice. You're brilliant, and I'm grateful for your friendship.

To my editor, Kim Bangs, you're the first person to say yes to my story. I'm not sure you'll ever know how much that meant to me. Thank you for giving me the opportunity to share the amazing things God has done in my life. I'm thrilled to be working with you! And even more, you like coffee maybe as much as I do. So that's pretty cool.

Thanks to the incredible Revell team for working so diligently to publish *Untangled*. I've always dreamt of working with a reputable house like yours, and am honored to be in the Revell family. May God continue to bless your work.

And a huge thanks to the beautiful and brave women who contributed to this book: Jenny Sulpizio, Jill Hart, Shanyn Silinski, Sarah Sams, Julie Thomas, Katie Birch, Karen Jenkins. I know it's risky to share your heart, and I appreciate your willingness to be vulnerable. Your stories have added such depth to my book.

But above all, I want to recognize my heavenly Father for his relentless pursuit of my healing. Thank you for never giving up on me, even in those seasons where I gave up on you. I'm humbled in knowing your eyes never looked away from my black and blue heart, and am grateful to be called your daughter.

Introduction

While I accepted Jesus as my Savior at a very young age, my faith has been a series of fits and starts. I often wondered if I really needed a savior, because life had shown me that nobody could protect me better than I could. If I couldn't trust men, how could I trust God? Where was he when evil came my way? What kind of God would let such things happen to a child? I began to see him as mean and uncaring, too busy with other more important matters than protecting me.

Youth groups were fun, but they weren't a place I'd meet God. Something might inspire me to recommit my life to him one weekend, but that "feeling" would fade come Monday morning. I'd wake up feeling just as worthless as the day before. Had he even heard my heart's cry for help? I began to think that God saved his time and energy for more worthy causes. And when people reminded me of his promise in Romans 10:13 to save those who called on God's name, I had trouble believing it. No one had ever saved me.

My college years and my twenties were experiments in pushing boundaries. All of them. Sweet mother. While I did have some rich seasons with God, most of the time I ran in the other direction.

I knew God existed, but I decided that if he didn't have time for me then I didn't have time for him. I'd spent years asking him to save me—to show me my worth—but nothing had changed. By then, so much shame and guilt covered me that I was certain I was just too messy.

But in my midthirties God's voice became louder than my brokenness. I started seeing just how relentless he had been in pursuing my healing. Sometimes it's easier to understand life looking backward. Hindsight is so very often 20/20. God had been there all the time. I just hadn't been willing to believe him.

I finally chose to believe that God's plan for me was better than the one I was walking out—quite a feat for a self-professed control freak with epic trust issues like me. But I was at the end of my rope, hopeless and joyless and bitter. Something needed to change.

God has been faithful to untangle those broken places in me ever since. For the past several years, those *not good enough* knots have loosened. I've been a tangled mess, but he is patient and gentle. My eyes have been opened and I have learned so much. I can see the part I've played through my bad choices, and I can also see how the Enemy has used guilt and shame to keep me tangled. And comparison has been one of his best tools.

I've been keenly aware of the successes and failures of those around me all my life. For a long time comparison was a measuring stick for how I was doing, and it was always very black and white. In my mind, I was either loved or unloved, approved or rejected, good enough or worthless. There has never been a middle ground. I might be easy to talk to and have a fun personality, a compassionate heart, great hair, and a good complexion, but I struggled with my weight—and that negated all good factors. With my fuzzy math, I was worthless no matter how I sliced it.

And while my husband still desperately tries to understand me when my crazy starts to show, but fails to get it, something tells me you understand perfectly. Because, girl, sometimes your crazy shows too. We all have that one particular tangle that knots us up, don't we? It could be weight, age, finances, parenting, marriage, health, friendship, the corporate ladder, or one of a million other things.

We see how easy and effortless that one thing is for *her*, and we come undone. The tangle tightens as we feel inferior, worthless, and incompetent. We may be rock stars in every other part of life, but that one pesky *not good enough* tangle totally knots us up. It has a way of overshadowing the truth of who we are, and whispers, *You'll never be worth anything.*

I've believed those words for years. So saying yes to God and writing this book about my story—my tangles—has been a very crunchy process. It's scary to be *that* transparent when you've spent most of your life as a chronic approval junkie. But with each word I write, the tangle seems to loosen just enough to encourage the next word.

Even getting this book published has been an untangling of sorts. Every rejection letter felt personal, like it was disapproval of *me*. But God used each no to help untie my knot of insecurity by teaching me to draw my sense of worth from him—not the world. Something I've never been able to do in my own strength.

These days, I don't need the world to love me like before. I've made peace with the knowledge that some may never approve of me, and I don't need their acceptance to feel like I matter. I'm okay with not being enough in their eyes, because I wasn't created to impress the world. I don't need the world to validate my message. God already has. And I'm at peace with not measuring up to the standards and expectations of others. Some are unreachable and others are just plain unsustainable.

But I'll be honest: I'm glad you're holding this book in your hands. I'm grateful you took interest in my story, and perhaps something stirred your tangled heart as you read the title. Maybe you can relate to the black and blue heart on the cover because it's how yours feels right now. Well, consider this your invitation from God to take a journey—one where he will restore your heart and untangle your self-worth so you can be who he created you to be. This book is God's reminder that he is in relentless pursuit of your healing too.

Jeremiah 29:11 tells us that his plans are for us to thrive. I didn't always see this promise daily, but I do now. And even when I cannot understand the *whys* and *not agains* that threaten to discourage and devalue me, I hold on to this verse. It offers me hope and reminds me that while the world is careless with my heart, God never is.

This book is my story—a story of restoration. God has taken me on a journey to untangle my knotted self-worth. He has opened my eyes to the lies that have kept me mangled in shame and guilt. He has straightened out my distorted self-image. He has been tender with my heart so bruised by the world. And God has revealed the truth of who I am because of Jesus: loved, accepted, clean, beautiful, approved of, and powerful. I'm beginning to understand that I'm an intentional creation, made on purpose and for a purpose.

And most of the time, I believe him.

This book is for anyone who thinks she isn't good enough. It's for the one who feels worthless and unimportant. I hope it will connect to the heart of any woman who is searching for significance, certain she won't ever measure up. My message is simple: you matter.

The world will look for ways to knock you down. The Enemy will always try to defeat you. And often your own thought life will keep you in bondage. But God is ready to untangle it all. Are you ready too?

I'm done giving Satan freedom to wreak havoc on my self-esteem. I'm done feeling like I will never be good enough. I'm done giving power to the people he used to hurt me, done with the situations meant to destroy me, done with all the evil he's unleashed in my life. Done. Done. Done!

It's taken me forty-three years to get to this point in my life, but I'm here now. For too long I have measured my value and worth by the world's scales. I've looked for affirmation and approval in the wrong places. I have spent my life striving to be good enough in the eyes of others. I've compared my worst with another's best.

The Enemy has had a heyday *with* me, but now it's a new day *for* me. Maybe for you too.

Chances are he's been using these same tactics in your life. And until we understand his plan to make us feel worthless, we'll find ourselves in a battle to keep our self-esteem from becoming a tangled mess.

Let me share what those knots have looked like in my life.

My *Tangled* Mess

Forty-three years after the abuse, I penned this letter:

To the man who molested me,
  You've been a part of my memory for most of my life. The things you said—the things you did—have tainted my ability to truly love myself.
  That day forever changed me.
  While I didn't understand what was happening, I unconsciously made an agreement with you about who I was, and who I should become. And since I've never been able to be that woman, I've struggled to be comfortable in my own skin. I've hated you for that. As I think back to that day, it's as clear in my mind this moment as it was forty-three years ago.
  It started out like any other day. I woke up happy. The world was good. Adults were safe. And evil didn't exist. And as I jumped on my tricycle, I had no idea I was peddling away from life as I knew it.

When I let my mind wander back, I can hear the sounds coming from the tools of the construction crew you worked with. I remember you taking my hand in the midst of the busyness and leading me into that apartment . . . closing the door behind us.

*I can feel the confusion and fear stir in my stomach now as I recall how you made me look at the images of naked women in a magazine. **And I remember your anger when I tried to look away.***

I remember how you escorted me from one room to another, closing yet another door to my innocence. When I shut my eyes, I can see you lifting me onto the ironing board. It seemed so out of place.

*I can conjure up the rush of emotions I felt in that room . . . **the ones telling me this was wrong.** And while I cannot bring your face into focus, I've never been able to blur out the way you touched me or the way you asked me to touch you.*

I remember how I screamed for help only to realize my voice never made it past my lips. But your voice did. I can recall, with great clarity, the words you spoke to me.

"This is your fault. If you tell anybody, you will be in trouble. You are bad and dirty and will never be worth . . . anything."

*Who **says** such a thing to a four-year-old? Who **does** such a thing to a four-year-old? And as you turned and walked out of my life forever, your words sank into me, took root, and became part of my DNA.*

*For most of my life, they've held such power over me. **I have wholeheartedly believed them.** I've struggled to feel beautiful—valuable. The words you spoke over me have been heavy weights of guilt and shame, dragging me deeper and deeper into a pit of worthlessness.*

I've hated you for that.

Sometimes I wonder if you remember me—if you recall what happened. Does it haunt you? Or have you buried it deep, distancing yourself from it? **Was I the first of many . . . or the only one?** *While our encounter may never cross your mind, it's forever etched in mine.* **But God has been unknotting the effects of that day.**

He is removing those words of hate you spewed all over me, and **replacing them with the truth of who I really am.**

He is untangling my self-esteem from the places you tied it, and **anchoring it in him** *instead.*

He is healing my little four-year-old heart, showing me that **I am good enough.**

He has **saved me** *from living a life of defeat and destruction.*

And while this process has been painful, and scary, and lonely, and long . . . **it's working.** *Psalm 34:18 [CEB] says* **"The Lord is close to the brokenhearted; he saves those whose spirits are crushed."** *I'm living proof of that.*

So I'm writing to tell you that you no longer have power over me. *Your words and actions are only a part of my past,* **not** *my future. So no matter what* **shame or guilt** *has been attached to that day,* **God has removed it.** *It wasn't mine to carry, anyway.*

Today I know I am beautiful. I know I hold great value in the eyes of my Daddy. I believe I'm more than good enough—I am powerful. And I'm greatly loved by the One who created me.

Because of those truths, what you meant for harm has been divinely trumped. And as a result, **I no longer hate you.** *Even more,* **I forgive you.**

But rest assured, there will come a day when **you will answer to my heavenly Father** *for the things you did to me. And justice will be served.*

Carey

19

While I didn't have a name or address to send the letter to, putting my feelings to paper was cathartic. I had no idea that abuse had tangled me up like it had. It was my ground zero, the place where everything in my self-worth changed. And for most of my life, I never made the connection.

For eight long years after it happened, I quietly carried the events of that day alone. When my perpetrator told me I'd get in trouble because it was my fault, I believed him. It was the perfect set-up by the Enemy. I kept silent, the feelings of worthlessness took root, and no one knew my self-worth was dying inside. By the time I shared it with my mom, those toxic beliefs ran deep and undetected. But looking back, it's easy to see how their effects manifested in different ways in every area of my life.

One of the biggest ways was in my ability to love and be loved. This has been a gaping wound for most of my life. I've struggled to trust that anyone could genuinely care for someone like me. After all, I was damaged goods—worthless. With all the girls in the world to choose from, why would any good man want me? I was always quick to remind myself that I wasn't pretty enough or thin enough. And so I settled for men who weren't a good match, sure I couldn't attract better.

I didn't trust the motives of men, either. In my opinion, they would say the right words to get what they wanted. When they proclaimed their love or complimented my outfit, it was all part of their evil plan. I was always just waiting for them to hurt me again, because that's what men did. At least that's what they seemed to always do to *me*. That mindset became a self-fulfilling prophecy—a tangle I wove myself.

But my insecurity wasn't restricted only to interactions with men. It also affected how I felt about myself, even around those closest to me.

When I was growing up, my family always spent Christmas with our relatives, who were scattered all over Texas. We'd take turns, one year at our house in Arlington, the next in San Angelo or Fort Worth or Houston. I loved visiting family at Christmastime. My cousins and I had a great time together. But I especially enjoyed our trips to Houston, where my favorite girl cousin lived. She was only a little older than me, and cooler than me by a mile.

Her bedroom was colorful, her closet bursting with the newest styles. The whole house was decorated to the nines—beautiful decor, classic furniture, plush carpet. It was a two-story home, something I'd always wanted. I envied her having a bedroom upstairs, away from the busyness of the family. Their cars were always nicer than ours, newer models with comfy leather seats. I would stare at the big homes in their neighborhood as we drove through the maze of streets toward their house. Wide-eyed, I'd notice how much fancier their community was than the one my family lived in.

Funny—I never thought we didn't have as much as they did until we visited them, and then it would become obvious to me. Painfully.

The hustle and bustle around the holidays was always fun in Houston. Looking at lights, playing dress up, baking cookies, eating the yummy fried pies my grandmother made, and going to the Christmas Eve service at a big church were always highlights. I loved those parts of our visit. But then came Christmas morning, and everything changed.

As the family gathered around the tree and distributed the gifts, my eyes would roam from the presents I had to the pile next to my cousin. She always had more than I did, or at least it seemed that way to me. I would keep tabs on each present as it was opened, noticing she got bigger and nicer things. I would feel the excitement of the holiday being crushed out of me under the weight of those comparisons. I was so jealous that she always had more.

One Christmas, her parents gave her a beautiful fur coat. Now I know it's not politically correct to like fur coats, nor is there a great need for that kind of warmth in Houston, Texas, but this one was gorgeous. I sat in envy as I watched her lift it from the

21

shredded ruins of wrapping paper and try it on. She twirled, everybody cooed with admiration, and my green-eyed little self was stuck in the trap of comparison. I felt worthless. Again. It didn't matter how great my gifts were, it seemed hers were always better. Good feeling gone.

In my mind, the number of presents under the tree was a visual representation of how much I was loved. And because the number was always (at least in my memory) smaller than my cousin's, it spoke volumes to me. While I was too young to know how much things cost, I knew there was a difference. The little bow-shaped earrings I got—which had topped my Christmas list—were cute, but they didn't hold a candle to that coat. When the last gifts had been unwrapped, my cousin stood there cloaked in luxury while I was wrapped in jealousy and the certainty that, like my gifts, I wasn't worth as much as she was. A tangle.

I knew in my little heart I was loved. My parents met my needs and we had a very comfortable life. We had fun as a family. We took vacations and spent quality time together. They went to all my sporting events and helped me with homework and school projects. I got sound relationship advice when I was struggling. They supported me and encouraged me to be my best. But the seed of *worthlessness* had already been planted, so the quantity and quality of presents under the Christmas tree were fertile soil for it to sink its roots into.

The *not good enough* belief ran deep. So much so that it flooded every area of my life, leaving me drowning in my craving to feel like I measured up to everyone else. And the waters of comparison continued to rise.

In high school I was an excellent athlete, and secretly wanted to be number one on the tennis team. I had the physical talent but lacked the belief that I had what it took to achieve that lofty aspiration. And no amount of encouragement from my parents or my coach could convince me otherwise. I tried out for the cheerleading squad—*more than once*—and never made it. But my friends did. I'd sit in the bleachers burning with jealousy, wondering what was wrong with *my* herkie jump. Or maybe my classmates didn't like me enough to vote me onto the squad. Regardless, it was another knot in a growing tangle.

When my college entrance exam score came back low, I never shared my disappointment. Instead I laughed it off, saying I preferred a party school over one that was academically tough. But if I had been honest, I would've admitted to being afraid of putting in the time and effort necessary to make a good grade. What if I did and still scored low? It would have proved I really wasn't smart enough, and I tried to avoid any situation that might confirm my fears. As my friends packed their bags for the bigger, more prestigious schools, I smiled and waved on the outside while hemorrhaging feelings of inferiority on the inside.

I came to realize that I always did just enough to get by, because being in the middle of the road was safe. Better to blend in with the pack than to try and fail. I didn't need another reminder—another validation—that I wasn't good enough. If I gave my best and fell short, the message of worthlessness couldn't have burned more if I had been branded with it. *You are bad and dirty, and will never be worth anything.*

I haven't lived a life completely devoid of hope. I wanted more out of life, and at times almost believed I was worthy of the dreams I had that would never quite die. But inevitably, every time I started to rise up and feel good about myself, my self-esteem would suffer another blow. The Enemy would whisper in my ear, reminding me of all the things I was supposed to be—but wasn't. *You will never be worth anything.*

For most of my life I've believed it—hook, line, and sinker. That message has run deep and wide inside me, undetected. And it's only been through this untangling season that I've seen just how damaging that belief has been. I've been trying to protect my little four-year-old heart every day since the abuse, trying in vain to convince myself that I was worthy. And it has cost me.

How many opportunities in life, how many chances at love, did I miss because I believed the words my abuser spoke over me? Looking back at a life that could have been lived better is sobering. But in helping me to do so, God has been unveiling where the Enemy has strategically tangled my self-esteem. And it's beginning to make sense.

I see why I'm easily triggered by the numbers flashing on the digital scale or those on the little labels sewn into my clothes. I understand why social media stats can ruin my day. I'm learning that these struggles don't measure the size of my heart, the complexity of my character, or the depth of God's love for me. When I see the age spots on my hands or the wrinkles on my face, I know why they sometimes upset me. I'm aware of the knots friendships cause, and how they've snared me more than a few times. But they don't define my value as a woman. I'm grateful for these "aha" moments, because they've helped loosen the knots of insecurity.

To be fair, sometimes seeking the world's approval has worked in my favor. There have been moments when I've received approval instead of rejection, value instead of worthlessness. There have even been instances where the world's stamp of approval has given me joy and excitement. I've seen God build my ministry from the ground up and shine his favor on it. I've been able to partner with different ministries, increasing my reach online. God has blessed me with good friends, filling my life with community. I have an awesome husband who has loved me enough to stick with me through very hard times. God has given us two beautiful children, even when medical experts promised we couldn't have any. Evil doesn't always win. But unfortunately, it's been a huge factor in tangling my self-worth and feeding my insecurities for years.

And not the only one. The tangles in my life have played out in many ways.

In My Finances

We're the poor folk of the family. Don't get me wrong; my husband and I make a good living, own a comfortable home, take vacations, and can stop at Starbucks regularly. But our financial resources pale in comparison to those of my parents and my sister and her husband. And although we're content with what we have, the reality is we can't keep up with them.

When we get together for dinners, holidays, or vacations, money is always on my mind. No one ever says or does anything to make us feel inferior; they are tremendously gracious and generous. I've got an amazing family. But because we can't write checks as big as they can, the lie I hear is that my husband and I are *less than* the others. We're the charity cases of the family. And even though I'm the oldest child, sometimes I struggle to feel like a grown-up. I often wonder if we're a burden, if they resent helping, or if the size of our bank account prevents the entire family from gathering more often.

I know their hearts and their genuine desire to bless us. I'm so grateful for them. When they say we repay them in other ways, I believe they mean it. And when they compensate for my family, they do so out of sincere love. I know this all to be true! But because I feel like a hindrance at times, accepting their help can be crunchy for me.

God recently showed me my underlying issue is shame, because at the core I don't feel like a success. I'm the one who works in the low-paying nonprofit sector and has a little ministry on the side. And because of it, I struggle with feelings of inferiority when I'm around my family. When the check arrives at the table and I know we cannot offer to pick up the tab for everyone's dinner, I'm embarrassed. And when one of them covers it all, I feel indebted.

In My Ministry

I do most of my ministry online because it allows me to reach across the world with what God has laid on my heart. I can interact with people from places I've never visited while sitting in my favorite chair. For this reason, I love technology.

After the last presidential election, I wrote a bipartisan blog post about our need, as Christ followers, to have a bolder presence in the world. So many laws and amendments had passed that directly opposed how God has asked us to live. My heart was heavy. But rather than complain about it, I encouraged my readers to be a louder voice for God. Not a voice of condemnation. Not one of anger or hatred. I challenged them to shine the light of Jesus in the world rather than sitting in silence, pointing others to God. It's what God tells us to do in Matthew 5:14–16.

"Regardless of who won," I wrote, "our purpose here on earth hasn't changed." That day I lost a noticeable amount of subscribers. Had I said something wrong? Frantically, I read and reread the day's blog post, searching for the offensive phrase. I couldn't find one. It wasn't disrespectful or unprofessional. My goal was to be encouraging, reminding that our job description as Christ-followers doesn't change based on who sits in the White House. Losing those subscribers hurt! Knowing they had opted out, the lie I heard was *What you think doesn't matter.*

Immediately I began to question my relevancy. Was I a good writer? Did I even have any business writing for God? I felt completely rejected by those people, strangers who had no idea they'd sent me into an emotional downward spiral. (Okay, so sometimes I'm a bit dramatic.)

My husband listened to me as I cried big tears of rejection. I hate when people don't like me. In my hurt, I wanted to throw in the towel and delete my blog. It just wasn't worth the heartache and rejection. Over the next few weeks, the loss of subscribers went from an annoying frustration to a battle with confidence. Who did I think I was anyway?

It changed how I wrote for a season. Rather than sharing authentically from my heart, I started writing "safe" posts no one could argue with. I felt guilty for writing that challenge, and shame for thinking I could.

In My Friendships

A few years ago, God clearly called my family to leave our church home of ten years. I fought it. This church was where my husband came to know Jesus. It was there that one of the pastors counseled our marriage back from the brink of divorce—more than once. This was the only church my kids knew, and they'd been to every summer camp it offered. My ministry was born there. It was where I first shared my story in front of an audience. My mentor worked at that church. My husband and I were deeply involved in volunteering, going on mission trips, participating in various ministry teams and committees, and so forth. I led women's Bible studies and we were both involved in individual and couples small groups. We were deeply invested.

So when God made it clear we were to leave, it wasn't something we did quickly or easily. We prayed about it at length. And even when we were certain God was telling us to move, we held on. We kept asking for more confirmation, and he kept giving it. God was so patient with us. But in the end, we reluctantly stepped out of the church. What came next completely floored us.

Our decision to do what God was asking angered some of my friends. I honestly never saw that coming. Weren't we taught to not only listen to God but also obey him? It never dawned on me that leaving the church would affect my friendships. So when several of my church friends distanced themselves or fell away completely, I felt so rejected.

Was I only worth their time if we worshiped under the same roof? I'd known these people for years. They were like family. We had walked many hard roads together, helped each other out in difficult situations. Our kids grew up together. These women knew my secrets. I had shared my heart with them. And when the friendship grew cold, it deeply hurt me. It was a very painful tangle because it reinforced those *not good enough* feelings that ran so deep.

I closed my heart off as protection. Rather than fight for the friendships, I decided to let it be. What if I fought and they still rejected me? It would reinforce how I already felt—worthless.

The lie I heard was that my value as a friend was conditional, that where I worshiped was more important than anything I had to offer as a friend. Ouch.

In My Marriage

From day one my husband was a big scorekeeper, God love 'em. If I went out with friends one week, it was his turn the next. If he changed a diaper, I was expected to handle the next one. When he made dinner, I was responsible for washing the dishes. He calculated everything, making sure we were even in both responsibilities and playtime. It was exhausting trying to keep up with whose turn it was and make everything fair. Nothing in life is 50/50.

I knew he kept track of the points in his mind and could remember whose turn it was at any given moment. It was suffocating, especially since I'd never been good at math. It left me feeling like a bad wife because he would get frustrated when the score tipped out of balance. How do you make marriage . . . fair?

Eventually his marital scoreboard made me angry, so I tried to keep score too. But I only succeeded in holding grudges and spewing my anger all over him. For those first several years, we camped out on divorce's doorstep. I lived in fear he would walk out on me at any moment. What kind of a wife couldn't make her husband happy? It reinforced my abuser's words. *You'll never be worth anything.*

My heart grieved because the *not good enough* messages were loud and proud. Why wasn't I worth fighting for? I longed to be cherished and loved and appreciated, but was scared to hope for those things. Based on my bad choices and shaky track record with relationships, I decided I was reaping what I sowed.

We've been married for fifteen years now, and thankfully, we threw away the scorecard long ago. We are better people now. A lot better. And I realize that God used our struggles to untangle some knots. We both had so many.

Today we have a rock-solid marriage, but every once in a while I feel the knot tighten. Isn't that life, though? My husband is an amazing leader and dotes on me and the kids like nobody's business. We've reached a level of trust in our relationship I've never known before—proof that God has untangled some very old knots. These days when Wayne tells me I'm beautiful, I actually believe him. Well, most of the time, anyway.

And as you'll see, the insecurities attached to the word *beautiful* are tangles deeply embedded inside me.

In My Femininity

In this area, life has been especially cruel. It's where my heart has been bruised the most. Comparison, jealousy, shame, guilt, rejection, and the message of *not good enough* have waged an epic battle against my self-esteem. This has been the hardest area for me to overcome. And to be honest, I am still working at it.

At one point during my time in the apartment, my abuser pulled a pornographic magazine from its hidden place and forced me to look at the pictures of naked women. I was only four years old, so my little mind couldn't process it all. But I realize the images on those pages have affected me more than I ever imagined. While I can't recall the pictures themselves, not in any great detail anyway, I knew these women were special somehow. They were important. And because my abuser had the magazine, I assumed men thought they were beautiful.

I was confused by all the thoughts and emotions swirling inside, and felt certain I could never be as valuable as the women who stared back at me. My abuser's words told me as much.

Those minutes were defining, because they formed my understanding of what the perfect woman should look like. I grew up believing I'd only be valuable if my curves were just so. If my stomach was flat and my chest wasn't, I would be adored. I had to be firm in the right places and bouncy in others. Beauty meant a small waist, big lips, and bigger hair. And on the inside, I had to be possessed with an insatiable need for sex. Um . . . right.

Here's the problem, though: I've never had the right combination of those things. None of us do, actually. Not even the women in the magazines, thanks to computer programs that nip and tuck to create the "perfect" woman. And because I lacked those qualities—in my mind those *prerequisites*—I've struggled with body image since childhood. I've never felt beautiful. Never. The scale, the tape measure, and the image in the mirror that didn't match up to the magazine images in my mind all conspired to make me feel downright ugly.

My mom has always said, "Aging ain't for sissies." Her Texas twang makes the words more believable, somehow, and her advice is spot-on. We live in a world that glorifies the young, the perky, the beautiful, and the skinny. And when we're not any of those things, or when we're not the perfect combination of all of them, the world quickly reminds us of it.

These days, I can't help but notice the number of wrinkles that have taken up residence on my face. My hair—one of the few physical qualities I've managed to feel good about my whole life—isn't as full as it used to be. My eyebrows are faint at best. I'm saggy,

I'm jiggly, and I'm noticing age spots on my face and hands. And as someone who struggles with all kinds of ideals associated with being a woman, my self-esteem can quickly tangle with insecurities.

In this area, I'm an easy target for the Enemy. He doesn't have to remind me of the women on the pages of that trashy magazine to make me believe the lie that I'm not desirable as a woman—I can just look at who and what the world worships.

When I get tangled up in these things, I hide. Literally. I put on the baggiest clothes I can find in my closet, usually a good pair of sweats. I don't reach out to my friends because I'm sure they'll notice a difference in me and want to talk about it. Rather than cry out to God for help, I will find ways to manage my own pain such as curl up in bed, find a good chick flick, and cry my eyes out. Alone. Sometimes it just feels too vulnerable to share those deep struggles with others. And when people reach out and ask if I am okay, I say I'm fine—keeping my broken heart in hiding too.

The *not good enough* tangles in womanhood have been my constant companions. They've made me doubt my worth, wondering if I have anything good to offer anyone. Those powerful messages have told me I'll never be as beautiful as the world says I should be. Sometimes I'm self-conscious about how I look and what I wear. The effects of aging can make me uncomfortable, and I wonder if they're as noticeable as they feel. And as much as I've tried to be content with how God made me, it's not always that easy. I've strived for approval and acceptance most of my life.

⁓

I've believed in God since I was a child. Jesus has been a part of my life as far back as I can remember—although sometimes I wanted nothing to do with him. I know and hear the Holy Spirit's voice. There are strong believers on both sides of my family, and many still attend church regularly. A few of my uncles were even pastors. I went to youth groups and summer camps, although mainly because of cute boys. My family prayed before meals and at bedtime. We even did family devotionals together. I grew up learning about my faith and how to walk it out.

I knew that God created me and Jesus died for me. I memorized verses that reminded me I was a new creation, a treasured possession. I knew with certainty that because of the cross, my sins were forgiven and my eternity secured in heaven. But this knowledge struggled to make the journey from my mind to the deep places in my heart.

Truth is, I never really believed I was important to God. How could I have been? If I really mattered, he would have saved me from that man—and the others that followed. God would have sheltered me from all the hurt and pain. He would have corrected the messages of worthlessness before they began wrapping around my self-worth and choking my confidence. Because, for heaven's sake, I was only *four*—an innocent child who did nothing to bring such evil her way.

Jeremiah 29:11 says, "I know the plans I have in mind for you, declares the LORD; they are plans for peace, not disaster, to give you a future filled with hope" (CEB). In his sovereignty, God knew evil would find me that day. And while he could've stopped the Enemy's plan, he didn't. That's been a hard reality to accept. I've been furious at him, screamed and cried at him, and turned my back on him, all the while wondering why he sat idle and did nothing. Weren't his plans for my life supposed to be filled with hope?

It's that kind of question that makes many people doubt the very existence of God. But not me. I have never doubted that my heavenly Father is real. But I have so many questions—the *whys*, the *hows*, the *why nots*. On this side of heaven I may never completely understand why God permitted the abuse. And when I get to heaven it really won't matter. But maybe—just maybe—he allowed it to happen because his plans were to also give me . . . *a voice*.

2

The First *Tangle*

The struggle for significance isn't a new one. It's not bound by gender, age, race, occupation, location, education level, or any other similar defining factor. While it might look different from person to person, everyone who lives and breathes on this planet will wonder, at one time or another, if they're *good enough*. It's a common tangle that weaves us together.

And the world offers plenty of ways we can attempt to detangle ourselves, doesn't it? According to a recent article in the *Boston Globe*, Americans spend close to $549 million each year on books promising to help them loosen the knot of insecurity.[1] These self-help books range from financial freedom to relationship success to weight loss.

So often, they put the burden of healing on us by saying, "You've got what it takes," or "It's all within your reach," or "For three easy payments of $9.99." We're encouraged to think positive thoughts and speak loving affirmations to the broken image staring back at us from the mirror. And unfortunately, we're no closer to seeing our value. As a matter of fact, the article goes on to share that many buyers of these books are repeat buyers.

Convincing us that change is within our ability alone is one of the biggest lies the Enemy whispers into our weary spirits. He tells us we don't need others and we most certainly don't need God. What we need, obviously, is that book and a huge helping of self-control. That's not been a record of success for me. How about you?

The reality is that we can't untangle this knot on our own. Believe me, I've tried. For years I gave it my best effort with counseling, cookies, control, church, community, and the like. But at the end of each day I wasn't any closer to feeling good about myself. The messages of worthlessness always screamed louder than any affirmation or encouragement I received from others. I was sure that if others really knew me, they wouldn't think I was that cool anyway. Sure, the Bible said God loved everyone, but I didn't think that included me. I never felt worthy of his time and effort. And no matter what I did to try and loosen the knots of insecurity that kept me tangled, I failed. I was certain I'd never be *good enough* for anything or anyone.

But I was missing an important piece of the puzzle. What I didn't understand was that God didn't feel that way about me at all.

I didn't understand how intentional God was in how he created me. I wasn't a rush job. He wasn't in a bad mood when he thought me up. I wasn't a cosmic collision or an accident. No, God created me on purpose—my quirks, my talents, my body, my challenges, my passions, my everything. He knew about the abuse and about all of the bad decisions I'd make, and he used them to train me. How do we learn to battle unless we're in one?

There weren't any deal breakers. I wasn't too messy. He decided when I'd enter the world and where I would live. He chose my family. He determined my kingdom calling. And according to Psalm 139:16, "The days of my life [were] all prepared before I'd even lived one day." The Creator knows me, planned me, and made me, and that makes me valuable—period.

In all thirty-one verses of Genesis 1, God creates. That chapter covers six days of God speaking heaven and earth into existence. He formed a whole bunch of nothingness into something beautiful for his soon-to-be prize creation, humankind. In Genesis 1:26, we enter into the world. And because God valued humanity above all else, he fashioned us into his own image. We are a reflection of our Creator. And in his opinion, he saved his best handiwork for last.

But here is my favorite part of the creation story. Verse 31 says, "God looked over everything he had made; it was so good, so very good!" From the beginning of time, we've held immeasurable value in his eyes. God has always considered us *good enough*.

It didn't take long, however, for insecurity to enter the scene and challenge that truth in our own hearts. In the next few chapters of Genesis, we discover how the knot of inadequacy wreaked havoc on a home, a marriage, and a woman, and set into motion a struggle that would plague every generation to come.

It's the first tangle. It's the story of Eve.

God's command to Adam in Genesis 2:16 was simple: "You can eat from any tree in the garden, except from the Tree-of-Knowledge-of-Good-and-Evil. Don't eat from it. The moment you eat from that tree, you're dead." So let's think about this. God gave Adam these instructions. He didn't write them down. They weren't posted online in the homeowner association covenants. No one else heard them but Adam. That's a pretty heavy piece of information, one that carries huge consequences.

But what you may not realize is just a few verses after this big-deal, life-changing, world-altering, earth-shattering command, God creates Eve. She wasn't even alive to hear those instructions straight from God himself. Adam would have to let Eve know.

It makes you wonder just how convincing Adam's directive was. Was it something like, "Hey Eve, so God doesn't really want us to eat fruit from that tree right there . . . okay?" Or was it more like, "Girl, if you eat from *that* tree, you will most certainly die!" This tidbit was, hands down, the most important mandate in the history of the world. And you can't help but wonder how she responded when he shared it. Did she blow him off, thinking he was being overly dramatic, or did she have every good intention of heeding his order? It doesn't take long to find out.

In the next scene, we find Eve minding her own business. She's hanging out, taking in all the sights the Garden of Eden has to offer. Can't you imagine? It was absolutely perfect. It wasn't too hot or too cold. The sun never threatened to burn. Cool water filled the streams and lakes. The animals lived in harmony. Spiders weren't allowed in (well, that may not be biblically correct). She was comfortable in her own skin, not worrying about stretch marks or wrinkles or cellulite or body odor. God's presence was everywhere, and she felt fully loved and valued and secure. Life was wonderful, her marriage was perfect, and Eve wanted for nothing. Until the serpent paid her a visit.

He begins the tangling process by asking, "Do I understand that God told you not to eat from any tree in the garden?"

Eve clarifies, letting the slippery serpent know that the rule only applied to the tree in the middle of the garden. The Bible doesn't give us a lot of details on the size of the garden, but we can assume it was thick with vegetation. And since they weren't yet meat-eaters (not even the animals), we can also assume most of the trees and plants produced food. Even if the garden was small and only had twenty-five different veggie, fruit, and nut options, they were free to eat all but one. Girls, wouldn't that make one heck of a salad?

The Enemy's question made Eve defend God's command— explain it away. And knowing human nature, it must have also planted a seed of doubt. Maybe she began to wonder why God would keep such yummy fruit from them. I imagine I might feel cheated, like I was missing out. It didn't matter that Adam and Eve could munch on every other plant in the garden. She couldn't eat from that one tree, and I imagine that began to eat away at her.

In September 2013, northern Colorado experienced a five-hundred-year flood. The Big Thompson River came roaring down the canyon and jumped its banks, leaving many communities in dire straits. At that time, we lived very close to the river and could see it, smell it, and hear it from our back deck. I've never been in a natural disaster before, and it was surreal. While our home didn't sustain any damage, the roads leading out of our subdivision were either washed out altogether or closed due to damage. We were trapped in our neighborhood for a few days, unable to leave.

Funny, my little heart is completely content sitting at home all day long and never leaving the comfort of our four walls. I am a homebody. But when the flood's destruction removed my freedom to come and go as I wanted, I desperately wanted out. I wanted what the local police told me I couldn't have. In a way, I can understand Eve's thought process. Instead of accepting the rule and trusting God's motives, Eve only saw what she couldn't have.

The cunning creature then goes in for the kill, making Eve doubt God's heart for her. "You won't die. God knows that the moment you eat from that tree, you'll see what's really going on. You'll be just like God, knowing everything, ranging all the way from good to evil" (Gen. 3:4–5). And just like that, Eve felt the pang of inadequacy. The message was simple: you're not as smart as you think you are. It whispered, *You're less than you could be.* Instead of being content with how God had made her, she wanted to be more. And knowing the only thing that stood between her and perfection was a bite of fruit proved too tempting.

At that moment, Eve wanted to be better. She wanted to be the best. So she took the bait, ate the fruit, and set into motion our age-old battle to feel *good enough.*

We don't have to look further than the Word of God to find countless examples of people who struggled with insecurities. They each had their own set of tangles that threatened to choke their self-worth to death. Most felt inadequate to do the job God called them to do. Some felt unworthy to have even been called. Several fell into the comparison trap, never feeling good enough about themselves. Others based their self-worth on their performance.

Rachel and Leah

Sibling rivalry makes for a great story, doesn't it? Hollywood has made millions pitting one sister against the other, especially when vying for a man's love. But we can find a real-life example in the pages of the first book of the Bible that is both beautiful and heartbreaking.

In Genesis 29, we're introduced to Laban and his daughters, Leah and Rachel. Leah was the older of the two, and the Bible describes her as having nice eyes. We're told that Rachel, her baby sister, was stunningly beautiful. With those descriptions, can't you just imagine how Leah might have struggled with feelings of inferiority? I mean, seriously. Having a sister of my own, I know it's easy to feel jealous when the other seems to have one up on you. This was undoubtedly the beginning of a tangled mess between these two siblings.

Many miles in the other direction, we meet Jacob. His father, Isaac, was trying to get his son settled into marriage. Instead of marrying his son to a woman from the local lot, Isaac sent him to find Uncle Laban, who just happened to have two single, eligible daughters. In those days, marrying within the extended family wasn't uncommon. And it's a good thing, because from the first moment they met, Rachel became the desire of Jacob's heart. And for the next seven years, he worked for her father to earn her hand in marriage.

The day had come for the two to be married, but Laban veiled Leah in deceit and sent her into the marriage bed instead of Rachel. So without Jacob knowing the change in plans, he consummated the marriage with Leah and fell asleep—and the sunrise brought a most unwelcomed surprise.

Imagine the beating Leah's self-esteem took when Jacob rolled over, opened his eyes, and found her in bed rather than his beloved *and stunningly beautiful* Rachel. Did he jump up in anger, screaming assorted expletives? Did he verbally berate her, reciting all the reasons he'd never marry someone like her, *nice eyes* or not? Maybe Jacob cried when he realized his seven years of work had been for naught. The Bible doesn't give us much information, but we can assume he was disappointed. And she must have been too. She wasn't what Jacob wanted, and it hurt.

But place yourself in her shoes for a moment. Don't you know that deep down she hoped for his acceptance? She wanted Jacob to see all the good things she had to offer. In those days, family was of the utmost importance and kids were essential to carry on the line. Leah must have longed for a husband and children. And as the oldest daughter she had expected to marry first, as tradition dictated. This was her time, and she would do anything to get it. Out of her insecurities she betrayed her sister, schemed with her father, and lied to Jacob.

But Jacob's love for Rachel was so great that he agreed to work another seven years for her hand in marriage. Can't you imagine how valuable this made Rachel feel? In his eyes, she was worth fourteen years of hard work. But imagine the jealousy that must have raged inside her too. The man she loved was now married to her sister. Each night of their honeymoon, Rachel lay alone in her bed wondering if anything was going on in theirs. And if so, was Jacob thinking of her during those intimate moments? Or worse, what if he was not?

I wonder if Rachel was afraid Leah might steal Jacob's heart. Looks can only take you so far, after all. And what kind of strain did it place on the relationship between the sisters? They were already struggling with their own insecurities, but the tangle was about to tighten even more.

When he'd completed his honeymoon week with Leah, Jacob married Rachel. Genesis 29:30 says, "And he loved Rachel more than Leah." Ouch. Tying her self-esteem to the affections of her husband, Leah felt unloved and worthless. But God saw her.

"When God realized that Leah was unloved, he opened her womb" (v. 31). God, in all his compassion and graciousness, gave her the ability to bear Jacob's children—something every man hoped for from a wife. Not only did this thrill Jacob, but it quieted the voice in Leah that told her she wasn't *good enough*. In the end, she bore him six sons and one daughter.

While Leah was a birthing machine, God had closed Rachel's womb. It would seem he was leveling the playing field a bit. The rivalry was heating up, and in Genesis 30:1 we see Rachel's insecurities reach epic proportions when she tells Jacob, "Give me sons or I'll die!" Wow, can't you hear the panic in her words? Rachel was tying her self-esteem to the ability to have children. She probably wasn't used to Leah having all of this positive attention either. But then things changed—again.

"And then God remembered Rachel. God listened to her and opened her womb. She became pregnant and had a son. She said, 'God has taken away my humiliation'" (vv. 22–23). Once Rachel's son Joseph was born, Leah's childbearing years came to an end. It was Rachel's time now.

These two sisters became bitter rivals for the love of one man, all tangled up in jealousy. Leah wanted what Rachel had, and Rachel wanted what Leah had. They were caught in the comparison trap—a trap designed to mangle the enjoyment of what they did have. And it worked, because the grass always looked greener by the other's tent.

When we are striving to meet our tangled desire to always be better than others, we'll never find contentment. We will be constantly comparing our worst with the best of another. We'll live lives full of envy, forgetting to appreciate what we already have.

As women, it's almost second nature. But these sisters show us how dependent our self-worth can become on our performance if we're not careful.

Hannah

How often do we find our sense of worth in getting something we want, thinking it will complete us? "If I just had a cuter figure, I'd be more desirable," or "If we lived in that neighborhood, I'd feel more important," or "If I was promoted to manager, I'd finally be respected at work."

We're certain that once we get our heart's desire, life will be wonderful, we'll feel valuable, and the emptiness will disappear. In our desperation to find significance, we look for validation in all the wrong places. We see this tangle play out in the story of Hannah.

In 1 Samuel 1, we learn how deeply Elkanah valued his wife Hannah. He knew how desperately she longed for a child, and was so tender with her heart. Verse 5 says, "He always gave an especially generous helping to Hannah because he loved her so much, and because God had not given her children."

But the rival wife, Peninnah, treated Hannah much differently. She felt superior because she'd been able to give Elkanah sons, and in her pride she ruthlessly taunted Hannah about her barrenness. Her attacks were cruel and often reduced Hannah to tears. Living in a time when children were expected, Hannah was left feeling inadequate and worthless.

Hannah's sense of value was tangled by her inability to become a mother, and it consumed her. She ached for children. And after ten years with no pregnancy, Elkanah took a second wife for the sole purpose of having children. Imagine how Hannah felt watching baby after baby being born to Peninnah. It was a painful reminder that she wasn't able to be the kind of wife she wanted to be—the kind of wife Peninnah was. She fell short and so she felt shame and guilt.

Although she was cherished by her husband and greatly valued in his eyes, she couldn't give him children. In her mind, a barren womb equaled a worthless woman. And that mindset tangled her self-esteem and negated all of her other blessings. Sometimes we let our desire for that "one thing" ruin us, don't we?

Elkanah was a godly man who saw right to the heart of his wife. In verse 8, he asks some pointed questions. "Oh, Hannah, why are you crying? Why aren't you eating? And why are you so upset? Am I not of more worth to you than ten sons?" It seems even Elkanah struggled with insecurity. In his mind, the love and kindness he showed her weren't good enough. His adoration and affirmations weren't able to help her overcome the sadness that consumed her. No matter how gracious he was, no matter how much he tried to make his feelings for her known, no matter how full of love his heart was for her, he couldn't make Hannah happy. Sometimes our tangles tangle others.

So often we forget that our insecurities can deeply affect those around us. Our family and friends might think they have the capability to make us feel better about ourselves, so they give time, encourage with words, and bless with stuff. And when they realize they can't mend us, failure whispers to them, *Your best effort isn't good enough.* Without meaning to, sometimes our inability to be "fixed" by those who love us can trigger feelings of inadequacy in them.

Elizabeth

So often, aging plays a factor in our insecurity. There are no shortages of creams and pills and procedures that promise to turn back the hands of time, restoring us to a *better* version of ourselves. We get tangled looking for the fountain of youth because the world says being young and beautiful matters most—not the gray hair and wrinkles of wisdom that come from living a full life.

The older we get, the less relevant we feel. Things sag, stretch out, and thin, causing us to feel self-conscious about how we look. We feel more fragile, becoming more cautious about the activities we engage in. We might say, "Oh, I'm just too old to do that," or "Maybe if I was younger." Our minds aren't as sharp or as quick as in our younger years, making us feel less capable. And all of these things have the ability to knot our self-esteem. Elizabeth offers us a great example of this.

In Luke 1, we meet Elizabeth and her husband, Zechariah. The Bible says they "lived honorably before God" (v. 6), but all that clean living didn't make up for the fact that she was barren. Barrenness was a common struggle in Bible times and it was considered a disgrace. But Elizabeth wasn't bitter toward God. She was old and past her prime childbearing years, but had learned to replace disappointment with faith. She loved God and trusted his plan for her life.

I can't help but wonder, though, if she struggled with feelings of being a failure—thinking there'd been a defect within her body that kept her childless. Or maybe wondering why God didn't find her worthy of having children. And how would it have tangled her self-esteem to sit on the sidelines as her friends and family were busy raising kids of their own? How many nights did she cry herself to sleep, feeling inadequate as a woman?

One day as Zechariah was in the temple doing his priestly duties, the angel Gabriel appeared and announced that Elizabeth was going to become pregnant. He listened as the angel shared all of the amazing things this child, soon to be John the Baptist, was going to accomplish. And rather than fall on his face in humility or jump up and down in elation, Zechariah's response was, "Do you expect me to believe this? I'm an old man and my wife is an old woman" (v. 18). Sometimes we can be a little cranky in our old age.

And just as the angel said, Elizabeth became pregnant. Instead of shouting it from the rooftops, she went into seclusion. Verse 24 says, "Some time later his wife Elizabeth became pregnant and did not leave the house for five months" (GNT). Commentaries agree that this might be because she wanted to make sure it was true before she announced the news in the town square. With her age, pregnancy was unheard of. She didn't want to proclaim it and risk embarrassment if it didn't come to pass.

As her belly began to grow, I would imagine so did her insecurities. Maybe she was worried about the rumor mill, afraid of what people might say. Maybe she was embarrassed by being pregnant at her age. She could have felt undeserving of God's great favor and answered prayer. Maybe she struggled to understand why God would trust her with this baby now, rather than in her youth. Regardless, Elizabeth tucked herself away from community for five months until her cousin Mary visited with the news that she was pregnant too. Both women were in scandalous circumstances. Sometimes we just need a friend to encourage us through our insecurities.

There's a common belief that says once we've reached a certain age, God retires us from service. The old gray mare is done, and now we're put out to pasture. But age means nothing to God. Whether we're one or one hundred, if we're breathing air on Planet Earth it's because we still have value and purpose for the kingdom of Jesus. We may feel worthless to God because there's no spring in our step or twinkle in our eye, but he never stops seeing our immeasurable value.

Saul

In 1 Samuel 9, we find the nation of Israel crying out for a king. This chosen nation didn't feel as good as other lands because their king wasn't of flesh and blood. And while God wanted to be the sole ruler of Israel, the nation didn't want him. They wanted to be just like everyone else.

To appease the people he called his "treasured possession" in Deuteronomy 7:6, God sent the prophet Samuel to find Saul, the man divinely chosen to be king. According to Scripture, Saul was "a most handsome young man. There was none finer—he literally stood head and shoulders above the crowd!" (vv. 1–2).

But sometimes no matter what we have going for us, we never feel like we measure up. When Samuel told Saul that he'd been chosen by God to rule the nation, he questioned it. In verse 21, he said, "But I'm only a Benjaminite, from the smallest of Israel's tribes, and from the most insignificant clan in the tribe at that. Why are you talking to me like this?" He couldn't believe that anyone, let alone God himself, would see leadership qualities in him. Even at the ceremony to introduce Saul as the nation's king, he hid among the baggage rather than stand proudly on stage.

During his entire reign, Saul's insecurities caused him to make tragic decisions, costing him God's favor and his own reputation. His biggest fear was looking bad in front of people—be it his subjects or his enemies. He was afraid to fail, needed public approval, feared humiliation, and battled pride. And Saul admitted it. "I've sinned. I've trampled roughshod over God's Word and your instructions. I cared more about pleasing the people. I let them tell me what to do" (1 Sam. 15:24).

Can you identify with this tangle? Sometimes we set aside what God wants from us because we're worried it might not be pleasing to others. Instead, we do what they find acceptable because their approval comes along with it. We worry that God won't give us what we need to do what he asks and we'll fail—big time. And for many of us, our tangled self-worth can't face another bout of rejection or embarrassment. It just isn't worth the risk.

Moses

God doesn't call the equipped, he equips the called. In other words, we aren't expected to have it all together before we do what God is asking of us. And it's a good thing, because God would be hard-pressed to find a candidate with those qualifications. He gives us what we need to do the work he places before us. Our job is to trust that he will. Even Moses struggled to believe it.

> The Israelite cry for help has come to me, and I've seen for myself how cruelly they're being treated by the Egyptians. It's time for you to go back: *I'm sending you* to Pharaoh to bring my people, the People of Israel, out of Egypt. (Exod. 3:9–10, emphasis added)

Moses, a shepherd minding his own business, had an unbelievable encounter with God that dramatically changed his job description. He'd still be a shepherd, of sorts, but God promised his flock would look much different. And when he heard this news, all sorts of insecurities popped up.

> Moses answered God, "But why me? What makes you think that I could ever go to Pharaoh and lead the children of Israel out of Egypt? . . . Suppose I go to the People of Israel and I tell them, 'The God of your fathers sent me to you'; and they ask me, 'What is his name?' What do I tell them? . . . They won't trust me. They won't listen to a word I say. They're going to say, 'God? Appear to him? Hardly!' . . . Master, please, I don't talk well. I've never been good with words, neither before nor after you spoke to me. I stutter and stammer. . . . Oh, Master, please! Send somebody else!" (3:11, 13; 4:1, 10, 13)

Moses was a tangled mess. He lacked confidence and was certain no one would believe what he had to say. And while Moses threw out every excuse in the book, God had chosen and would not be dissuaded. Moses had no choice but to step out in faith, trusting that the great I AM would be with him through it all. And he was. Moses did the job placed before him, and did it well.

Can't you relate to him, though? So often we feel completely inadequate to do what God has asked of us. We get tangled up in all the reasons we *can't* rather than trusting God for the reason we *can*. It's not about our weakness; it's about God's strength.

We also find insecurities in Timothy, who felt unqualified to lead because of his young age. Gideon was insecure about the battle plan God downloaded to him. David feared evil, often pleading for God to remind him of his protection. Sarah struggled to feel like a good wife because she couldn't get pregnant. Rahab felt worthless, seeing prostitution as her only career option. Shall I go on?

Truth is, we could look at every biblical character and find insecurity, just like we could look at our friends and family and find the same. It's important to know that we aren't alone in our *not good enough* feelings and that God isn't repulsed by our insecurities. He sees the potential of who we will be, rather than only focusing on who we are now.

From the first lady on Planet Earth to you and me, the struggle to have a healthy self-esteem connects us. It weaves us all together. And while we may see our flaws as deal-breakers, God never has—and never will. Instead, he puts a purpose on each of our lives regardless of how broken we are inside. I love knowing that. Only God can look past our messes for our messages.

The *Tangled* Expectations of Women

"Mom, look at this." As we sat at the coffee shop one day, my then-ten-year-old daughter started sketching out her wedding dress. It was meticulous, from the veil to the shoes. She took its design and functionality into consideration, hoping her ceremony would take place on a beach. I loved watching her excitement as she dreamed of the flowers, bridesmaids' dresses, music, and even the name of the one who would steal her heart. It was obvious this wasn't the first time her big day had danced through her mind.

She shared her ideas about the ceremony itself, from the seating arrangements to the song her soon-to-be-husband would write *and* perform for her in front of a teary-eyed crowd. We talked about which beaches she'd consider for the wedding and what the honeymoon plans might include—either staying on the island or leaving from there on a monthlong cruise. My baby likes to go big or go home.

I was never one of those girls who dreamt about her wedding day with such detail. I didn't think about what kind of dress I'd wear or what color combinations worked best together. I never considered the flavor of cake or how the designer would adorn its layers. I didn't wrestle with the decision of who I'd want as bridesmaids or mull over what types of flowers they'd carry down the aisle. I never created a "pros and cons" list for a church wedding versus a beach wedding. But my friends did, and I'd sit and listen, nauseated at the thought because I was certain no one could really love me. Refusing to detail out my wedding was a coping mechanism, because it kept my heart safe.

But as I sat with my daughter that day, God revealed something to me. *My girl wanted to be celebrated.* At the very core of her elaborate plan was the desire to feel special and beautiful and *seen*. And while I had covered my heart and ignored my pain for most of my life, the truth is I had wanted those same things too.

Somewhere in your life, you've also made these kinds of agreements. The ones that redefine who you are—and who you are not. The ones that make you question your goodness and tell you your differences are a defect rather than a delight. Those agreements keep you from seeing yourself as God sees you. These are the lies we internalize as truth, the ones that say *you'll never measure up*. The ones that usually become self-fulfilling prophesies.

See if any of these sound familiar:

I am a fraud, and if people really knew me they would see I'm not as smart/friendly/faith-filled/talented/loving/_____ as they think.

I am either too much or too little, never just right.

My value to men is based on the measurements of my body.

I'm not worth anyone's time or effort.

I'm lucky to be loved.

No one will ever be able to love me because I am broken.

I will always be second best, so I shouldn't even try.

My weight determines my worth.

I'm only as good as my next achievement.

There is no one I can trust.

I must control others before they control me.

I am not good enough to be friends with those women.

At my age, I'm no longer relevant.

I'm embarrassed to let anyone see where I live.

No matter what he says, I know my body is unattractive to my husband.

Because my kids fail, I'm a failure.

If I just had more money I'd be happy.

These lies resonate with some very deep places in me because I've believed every one of them at some point in my life. I've used them to define my self-worth. They've made me wonder if I hold any value to those around me—if I really matter to anyone. And even worse, I adopted them as truth and they became a part of me. I wonder what lies you would add to the list.

Well, here's where the tangle tightens. We allow these agreements to become our new reality, or well-deserved punishments, or even safety measures to protect us. But at the very core, they are lies. And they become bricks in the wall we build around our hearts to keep people from seeing the real us—the *us* we're certain isn't good enough. We hide our feelings of worthlessness.

If you're breathing air today, you have walls. We all do. We're all guilty of partitioning off our hearts so we don't get hurt anymore. Walls shouldn't be confused with boundaries, because establishing healthy limits with toxic people and beliefs is smart. Boundaries are proactive, but walls are protective. Boundaries help us live within community, but walls keep us from it. Boundaries are put in place for healing, while walls are built to hide our hurting. Walls are boundaries gone bad, and their bricks are made from feelings of rejection and inadequacy. But that's not how God wants us to live.

You and I weren't created to hide ourselves. Matthew 5:14–15 confirms it. "You are the light of the world. A city on top of a hill can't be hidden. Neither do people light a lamp and put it under a basket. Instead, they put it on top of a lampstand, and it shines on all who are in the house" (CEB). Without a doubt, God created us to be seen.

He wants his glory in us to shine to the world. And even though the presence of sin in ourselves and in the world has caused us to function in ways we were never meant to, the Creator sees us through the righteousness of Jesus. His blood covers us. It's made us clean. Because of that, God sees us as magnificent. We were made on purpose and saved on purpose, and God celebrates his creation.

Sometimes it's hard for me to reconcile that I'm *enough* for him. How can I be? There are so many things about me that are not beautiful, and plenty of reasons not to celebrate who I am. I have mean thoughts, I say hurtful things, I judge others and judge myself, and I fall into the comparison trap more often than I care to admit. I pretend to be things I'm not, hoping to impress. My motives can be underhanded, and sometimes I seek the approval of man instead of the approval of God. I can operate out of shame and guilt, bleeding my insecurities all over others. Sometimes I'm prideful, lacking any true humility. And I can live with a sense of entitlement.

But regardless of my human condition, Psalm 103:11–12 says God loves me anyway. "Because as high as heaven is above the earth, that's how large God's faithful love is for those who honor him. As far as east is from west—that's how far God has removed our sin from us" (CEB).

Wouldn't it be nice to live as if we believed those words? We read them, we know God loves us and forgives us, but the reality doesn't weave its way into our DNA. For most of us, the eighteen-inch journey from the mind to the heart is a road less traveled. What would happen if we let that Scripture wrap around us and anchor in our black and blue heart, reminding us that his love is deeper and bigger than our insecurities? What if we believed we are who God says we are: precious, beautiful, accepted, powerful, capable, approved of, and a treasured possession? What would happen if we knew beyond a shadow of a doubt that we mattered greatly to our Creator? Well, it would change everything. And the Enemy knows it.

The accuser's voice, telling us that perfection is expected, never lets up. He is clever to find the exact way to knot us up in our *not good enough* feelings every day. Satan knows precisely what will trigger us. He and his minions design situations to make us doubt our magnificence and significance. The Enemy's voice is loud, and the world is his speaker. And the *you'll never measure up* messages that constantly bombard us are all tainted with one power-packed emotion—shame.

Shame. It's that five-letter word that feels more like a four-letter word. According to Carl Jung, "Shame is a soul-eating emotion."[1] It's real and it's a doozy, and I'd like to suggest it is the foundational emotion that fuels our feelings of worthlessness.

Think about it. Guilt is the feeling of *doing* something wrong, and shame is the feeling of *being* something wrong. This emotion surfaces when we're in situations that embarrass, dishonor, disgrace, or humiliate us. We feel it when we continue to sin, unable to break the cycle. Shame happens when our inadequacies are exposed and we think others are negatively judging us. We become overly sensitive or fearful of rejection and criticism, and so we withdraw, certain we're the problem.

Shame can look different too. It might show up as anger or embarrassment when our *not good enough* shows, or look like pride when we act as if nothing bothers us. We might become fearful of situations that would highlight an inadequacy, so we avoid them altogether. But under it all, we feel that something is fundamentally wrong with who we are. And that shame affects how we feel about ourselves at the deepest level. This life-draining emotion started in the Garden, with a bite of the forbidden fruit.

> And as they ate it, suddenly they became aware of their nakedness, and were *embarrassed*. So they strung fig leaves together to cover themselves around the hips. That evening they heard the sound of the Lord God walking in the garden; and they hid themselves among the trees. The Lord God called to Adam, "Why are you hiding?" And Adam replied, "I heard you coming and *didn't want you to see me* naked. So I hid." (Gen. 3:7–10 TLB, emphasis added).

The first couple was riddled with shame, insecure about their nakedness, and worried about being judged by God. Instead of running to him for validation of their worth, they hid. They were afraid of what he might think of them now.

For most of my life, I've hidden behind a wall of shame. I built it with bricks made of lies such as *You're not good enough*, or *You're different than they are*, or *You don't have what it takes*, or *If they only knew*, or even *They'll see right through you and realize you are nothing special*. Until recently, I didn't recognize that voice as shame. I'm not even sure I knew there was a voice I was listening to.

Shame is at the very root of your feelings of worthlessness, but it has an uncanny way of disguising itself as something else, or even hiding altogether. It's very dangerous to your self-esteem because no matter what you do or how hard you try, you never feel like you're good enough. It can be triggered three ways.

> Not living up to your own standards. *I didn't want to gain weight over the holidays but I did anyway! I failed again.*

Not living up to the standards of another person. *My husband wants to be more intimate but I am so tired at the end of the day. I'm always letting him down.*

A circumstance. *I can't believe I yelled at my kids again. I'm a horrible mom and they deserve better.*

Shame dangles the proverbial carrot of acceptance in front of us, encouraging us to work for the approval of others. It tells us to control everything and everyone so our inadequacies stay tucked away. Shame's voice says that when we're people-pleasers, others will recognize our servant's heart and we will be loved. Shame suggests we judge others to make ourselves feel superior. It tells us to withdraw from community to avoid painful reminders of our *not good enough*. Shame reminds us to keep our mouth shut because no one wants to know what's really on our mind or in our heart. It cautions us to be agreeable so others can't see us as difficult. Shame suffocates us.

Can I be honest? I was well into my forties before I recognized the role shame played in my life. So, sister, if you are just now connecting the dots and finding shame in your life too, you're in good company. I had no clue how tight the tangle of shame had been woven throughout my self-esteem. The Enemy has been clever in hiding it. And because I rarely struggled with guilt, I assumed shame was the same thing. But it isn't—not at all.

We feel guilt for *what we do* and shame for *who we are*. And the Enemy targets our womanhood because he wants us to be ineffective. As women, we hold a great deal of power and persuasion. We are wives and moms, daughters and friends. We have jobs and run companies. We are so often the glue that holds relationships together. And if the Enemy can shake our confidence and make us second-guess our value, it can have ripple effects now and for generations.

Our Appearance

I've worked for a faith-based nonprofit organization for close to fifteen years now. Each year we hold a fundraising banquet where we invite our donors to come celebrate God's faithfulness to our mission. We have a silent auction, serve a yummy dinner, and present a short program highlighting the year. It's a very big deal. It's also a formal occasion.

The staff and volunteers arrive early the day of the event. Most of us are in sweatpants and sweatshirts, without an ounce of makeup, our hair in ponytails. We all have different assigned tasks as we run about preparing the room for the night. It's a flurry of activity, but we all really enjoy being together. The preparation might be my favorite part of the event.

About an hour before the guests arrive, we all squish into the bathroom to get dolled up for the night. One year, the women were talking and giggling as usual, and I listened as everyone began complimenting each other. So-and-so's lipstick was the perfect shade of red. Her dress was simply elegant. Those heels made her legs look terrific. Her hair had never been cuter. That shawl was an awesome find. And the compliments kept flying around the room. Except not one came my direction. While I know this omission wasn't on purpose, it still hurt my feelings. It made me self-conscious because I wondered what was wrong with how I looked.

No other tangle is as common to women as this one. The pressure to be beautiful is one of the biggest knots in our self-esteem. On average, we see about two thousand ads a day telling us what we should look like and who we should be.[2] And the ad campaigns are working, because the average woman will spend about $15,000 on cosmetics in her lifetime, with $3,770 being for mascara alone.[3] I totally get that. It's the one cosmetic I wear every day, rain or shine.

Another study found that approximately 91 percent of women don't like their bodies, and they diet in hopes of finding a way to feel good about the way they look. That leaves only 9 percent of women feeling good about their appearance.[4] If we grew up being told that beauty comes from within, we're certainly not buying into the idea today.

We can't ignore the huge influence media has on how we feel about ourselves. Movies, television shows, magazines, and the internet bombard us with body images that are unrealistic and unsustainable. Their example of how we should look isn't attainable. These images are the product of perfect lighting, creative makeup, selective airbrushing, and remembering to "suck in their gut" at the right time. These picture-perfect women we idolize for their beauty have a posse of others to make them look flawless—hairstylists, makeup artists, personal trainers and chefs, wardrobe designers, and the like. With help like that, any of us could razzle and dazzle. And the beauty industry knows that if we feel bad enough about how we look, we'll try their products as a remedy.

Cosmetic and clothing companies spend billions of dollars each year reminding us we're not young enough, skinny enough, or sexy enough. We have too many wrinkles and fine lines. Our lips aren't plump enough and our eyelashes aren't long enough. When we walk, our back ends jiggle too much. When we sit, our thighs spread out too much. Our skin is either too dull or too shiny, and our hair lacks luster. This bra will make us look perkier and these jeans will make us look smaller. And if we wear this brand of panties, no one will know we have any on at all. Since when is wearing underwear a crime?

My daughter recently got a catalog in the mail from a well-known tweener clothing store, and as I thumbed through the pages I got angrier and angrier. Apparently what is all the rage these days is having a gap between your thighs so they don't touch. Girl, I don't remember the last time mine didn't. I found a few images where it was easy to see the graphic designers had airbrushed a gap that wasn't actually there. It made the girls look dangerously skinny, sending the message that thin is not only in . . . it defines beauty. I picked up the catalog and threw it in the trash. And I might have said a bad word.

Advertising firms also use slogans to tangle us. They work overtime to find the perfect wording to prompt us into action. Their goal is to poke that deep place inside that says *you could be better* and offer their product as a solution. Below are a few examples. This list includes both recent ad campaigns and a few that are a blast from the past.

L'Oréal—*Because You're Worth It*

Maybelline—*Maybe She's Born With It, Maybe It's Maybelline*

Camay Soaps—*You Are in a Beauty Contest Every Day of Your Life*

Clairol Hair—*If I've Only One Life Let Me Live It As a Blonde!*

Listerine Mouthwash—*Her Honeymoon—and It Should Have Been Mine!*

Body Bra by Warner's—*Do You Want a Shape Like a Bra? Or Do You Want a Shape Like a Woman?*

Levi's Jeans—*Have You Ever Had a Bad Time in Levi's?*

Maidenform—*I Dreamed I Stopped Traffic in My Maidenform Bra*

Max Factor Cosmetics—*To Bring the Wolves Out—Riding Hood Red*

Pretty Feet Deodorant—*What's the Ugliest Part of Your Body?*

Roxanne Swimsuits—*Some Girls Have Developed a Lot More Than Just Their Minds*

And my all-time favorite: *The Most Unforgettable Women in the World Wear Revlon.* They may be on to something, though. I don't use their brand of makeup and people forget my name all the time. This slogan just might be true.

To tighten the tangle of insecurity, the body type used in advertising portrays only 5 percent of American females.[5] We're led to believe the images we see are of the ideal woman, and it is a look the vast majority of us cannot achieve.

As women, we're measured against an impossible yardstick all the time. More times than not, we come up short. The world may remind us and others might tell us, but so often we are the voice that convinces ourselves we're not good enough. How many times have you seen a print ad where the swimsuit model has zero percent body fat? Not an inch of skin bulges over her suit. And when you notice that your skin bulges over in a few places, you beat yourself up. We're our own worst critic, and our internal dialogue is brutal.

When was the last time you called yourself ugly? Can you recall telling yourself you'll never be good enough for him? Have you ever called yourself stupid for trusting that person, or made some snide comment about your weight when shopping for clothes? Do you cuss yourself out when you make a bad decision, or talk yourself out of accepting affirmations from others?

Proverbs 4:23 says, "More than anything you guard, protect your mind, for life flows from it" (CEB). Did you catch that? More than *anything* else, protect your mind. You see, when you undermine your worth through your words and thoughts, you change how you see yourself. You change how you respond to the world. You live life reflecting on your worthlessness.

For most of my life, I've hated my body. Even at my very fittest, I saw so much room for improvement. I've tried speaking positive affirmations into the mirror—"Dang, girl! You are looking good today!"—but it always felt awkward and I struggled to believe it. I might be having an excellent hair day, but the jiggle in my arms unnerves me. Or my skin might be clear but I notice one eye is smaller than the other and I'm self-conscious about it the rest of the day. Nowadays, I can't help but notice the wrinkles and sags.

It's a battle we can't win. There's not enough time in the day to do all the things we're supposed to do to be beautiful. While advertisers and Hollywood may make it look easy, it's not. And because we can't achieve the results we want, our self-esteem takes a hit. Most of us aren't able to be comfortable in our own skin.

Our Age

You'd think that after a certain age, we wouldn't obsess about our flaws. At some point, shouldn't we make peace with our imperfect bodies and embrace the bumps and sags and stretch marks? Yes. But because the world worships youth, we spend millions of dollars trying to hold on to it.

A study from the *International Journal of Eating Disorders* revealed that women over fifty still struggle with body image. Of the 1,849 women over fifty surveyed, 62 percent said their weight or shape had a negative impact on their lives and 66 percent were unhappy with how they looked.[6] And many of us are doing something drastic about it. According to the American Society of Plastic Surgeons, Americans spent $11 billion on face-lifts, Botox injections, breast augmentations, and other elective cosmetic procedures in 2012.[7] In an effort to feel more confident and beautiful, we're paying big bucks to physically alter the way we look.

Wanting to look our best isn't a crime. Sometimes we need surgery to correct an issue. But so often we do it for the wrong reasons. We think wrinkles and crinkles make us less of a person, like we aren't as important as when we were younger. The late actress Lauren Bacall once said, "I think your whole life shows in your face and you should be proud of that."[8] That's sound advice. We cannot stop the aging process, but we can stop letting it negatively affect our sense of value.

Our Health

Some of us satisfy those *not good enough* feelings through our health and fitness levels. We allow our body fat percentage, the number on the scale, our cholesterol level, how fast we can run a mile, or a clean bill of health at our annual physical to determine how we feel about ourselves.

We brag about our latest workout, post pictures of the low-calorie dinner we made, share our measurements online, or comment about how many flights of stairs we walked so others will affirm our "good choices." And when they affirm our efforts, we feel better about ourselves.

An article titled "The Heavy Price of Losing Weight" revealed that Americans spend more than $60 billion each year on gym memberships, weight-loss programs, and diet foods.[9] Wanting to look and feel our best isn't a bad thing in and of itself, but sometimes we take it to unhealthy levels. When it becomes a way to garner the approval of others, that's a waving red flag that we've crossed a line.

At an event I was speaking at a few years ago, I shook hands with a woman and asked how her day was going. She replied, "Great! I ran five miles this morning and the scale showed I lost those pesky two pounds. I'm good again!" As she stood there smiling at me, my heart broke. I wanted to hug her and whisper all the reasons she didn't have to prove her worth, but I knew that conversation would be longer than we had time for.

You are not the sum of the miles you've run or the calories you eat. Your worth isn't based on how much you weigh or the number of times you hit the gym each week. And when we let those things define us, our worth becomes dependent on approval.

Our Sexuality

Today's reality is that sex sells, and advertisers use it to entice consumers to buy whatever it is they're selling. While it may boost sales, portraying women as objects is wreaking havoc on our self-worth. Why? Because we're being conditioned to think that being sexy equals being esteemed. Not only that, but it changes how men see us, what they want from us, and the value we hold in their eyes.

Men's magazines like *Maxim* have capitalized on the sex sells concept, often using half-naked women on their covers to attract attention. In one experiment, they found the issues that featured a sexy woman on the cover outsold the issues showing a man, even if the celebrity or athlete was someone of interest to the buyer.[10] The bottom line is that media is using us to sell their product, and we aren't objecting.

You need look no further than the checkout line at the grocery store, television commercials, prime-time television shows, or the storefronts of clothing retailers to see that our sexuality is being used for profit. And women can get something in return for allowing men to fantasize about their bodies. It can make them feel beautiful and desired and can also pay well, and that translates into feelings of worth.

Unfortunately, that attitude is trickling down to you and me. Why? Because media and culture have told our men that we should be sexier. So we are becoming more willing to do things and try things—some way out of our comfort zones—to satisfy them. And when the response we get from men is so overwhelmingly positive, it can feed our craving for adoration even if we feel compromised because of it.

The common message weaved through it all is that to be prized and treasured you must be a super sexy, tight-clothes-wearing, want-it-all-the-time, up-for-trying-anything-at-least-once sex kitten. I don't know about you, but none of that describes me. As a matter of fact, I've never met a woman it does describe.

We may not be the sultry woman portrayed on the magazine cover and we feel bad about it. We may push through our concerns and try new things to satisfy our men, but then we feel cheap and used. And when we see the perfect images of women in the media, we can't help but compare their best features with our worst features and come out feeling *less than*.

Our Social Calendars

My husband and I rarely get invited to parties or asked out to dinner. Oddly that never bothers me—until I hear of other couples getting together, and then I start wondering what's wrong with us, or more pointedly with *me*.

We love a good time with friends and enjoy getting out. I think we're easy to get along with, especially my husband. My man and I don't have some infectious disease, or do embarrassing things in public—at least not on purpose. Well there was that one time that I laughed so hard I snorted, and the entire restaurant stopped talking and looked my direction. And we did forget our wallets once, causing our friends to foot the dinner bill. Oh, and there was also the time that I didn't see the step down from the booth and I fell flat on my face. Those are common faux pas though, right?

But for some reason, most of our weekends are spent at home hanging with the kids. We catch up on television shows, sleep in, and work our way through those endless to-do lists. And while that's all good and necessary, sometimes I feel left out and worry that I'm not as in-demand as others.

Life today moves at a much faster pace than in previous generations. We pride ourselves on busyness. The world tells us to *do* more and *go* more, and we've bought into it. And while we sometimes complain about our full calendars, oftentimes we secretly love the flurry of activity because it makes us feel popular. It's become a bragging right of sorts. We feel important when our weeks are filled with meetings and outings and activities. And for some of us, an uncluttered calendar points to an insignificant woman.

Wanting to engage in community is exactly God's plan for us. We were designed to spend time together. But when we allow the fullness of our calendars to determine how much we are valued by others, we can be certain it's unhealthy.

Our Faith

Have you ever been afraid to pray out loud in front of others because you're worried your prayers aren't as good as someone else's? Or maybe you are self-conscious about sharing your insights at Bible study because you're certain the other women will find your comments silly? We can get so trapped in comparison when it comes to our faith.

I've led small groups and Bible studies off and on for years. And in every one of them, I've known one or two women who have felt terribly inferior. It's understandable. Many of us would admit to being hurt by the church at one time or another. We've seen women who think they're better than the rest of us. We've heard the flowery prayers—the ones where they sound super holy but we really have no idea what they're even saying. There have been others who were very judgmental or condescending. Many of us have been corrected in front of a group in a mean-spirited way. And it's left us feeling insecure about connecting with other women and sharing our thoughts or prayers out loud.

Why are we afraid to say something wrong? It's embarrassing. What's the matter with having a different opinion? Ours might not be popular. Why won't we pray out loud? We might sound silly. The body of Christ is losing confidence to thrive in community because we're worried a misstep in our thoughts or our words indicates stupidity. And we desperately want to be liked and accepted.

But you know what? God created each of us differently and gave us unique gifts and talents and insights. We're all pieces of a big puzzle. We're each formed differently. So when you decide not to share your heart in community, we all lose out.

Your self-worth isn't dependent on being Miss Holier-Than-Thou. You aren't better or worse for having questions about theology. Your significance isn't based on how many verses you've memorized. And using big and flowery words doesn't make your prayers more influential.

Can we agree that it is hard being a woman in the world today? We all have reasons for being tangled up in the knots of insecurity. Maybe you, like me, have suffered sexual abuse that has you covered in shame. Maybe you've grown up being told you'll never measure up. Maybe you've succumbed to the pressure of wanting to be thinner, richer, smarter, younger, sexier, or holier, and it's left you feeling even worse about yourself. Maybe your internal dialogue berates your self-esteem every day with reminders that you'll never be what anyone needs. Regardless of its cause, insecurity is a common thread that weaves us together. But friend, God has a different message.

He loves you right now, right here in your tangled mess—your stumbles, fumbles, and all. And there is nothing you can do to make God love you more or less. Your tangles don't intimidate him. They don't scare him off. Romans 8:38–39 confirms it:

> I'm absolutely convinced that nothing—nothing living or dead, angelic or demonic, today or tomorrow, high or low, thinkable or unthinkable—absolutely nothing can get between us and God's love because of the way that Jesus our Master has embraced us.

Just like my daughter dreams she'll be on her wedding day, I've wanted to feel special, beautiful, and seen, but I've never felt worthy of it. But through the untangling of my womanhood, God has revealed the truth of how worthy I actually am. And when you ask, he will do the same for you.

Her Tangle: A Story from Karen

Intimacy. I'll assume I am not alone when I say this word brings up a tangled web of emotions. And being a broken woman with wounds that run deep, intimacy has always been a struggle for me.

I used to think it only meant a romantic relationship, like with my husband. But in the dictionary, that definition is listed *third*. The first definition is much broader. It means a closeness or a loving, personal relationship with another person or group. This means that in every relationship we have, intimacy can make it better. But it also makes it trickier.

Sure, we may have friends who we shop with, have a glass of wine with, exercise with, or talk about parenting struggles with, but do they really know our heart? We have husbands who love us, and whom we love back, but can they really understand what makes us tick? Finding someone who loves you for *you* is a gift. And when you find that kind of intimacy, it bolsters your self-worth. But when it seems like an endless challenge, it makes you wonder what's wrong with you.

Maybe you don't, but I know exactly why I struggle with it. As a little girl, my innocence was stolen by my stepfather. Brutally. But all memory of it was repressed until I was thirty-seven, when the sexual intimacy of marriage began to overwhelm me. Slowly and painfully, the memories of my abuse began to come back, leading me straight into the darkest time of my life.

Counseling saved my life, and Jesus held me through it. With time and revelation, things began to make sense. Suddenly all my hang-ups, insecurities, and feelings of worthlessness had a source. And because the abuse had confused my idea of intimacy, I realize how very inadequate I'd felt most of my life.

While my mom had an idea something was going on, and that it related to my stepfather, I didn't reveal anything to her during the counseling. I was so tangled in shame. But when I finally did, I remember it with great clarity.

As I shared my journey, she sat and fiddled with her hands. Her face was devoid of emotion. She didn't speak more than two words at a time. And after what seemed like an endless amount of awkwardness, she stood up, hugged me, said she believed me and was sorry, and walked out the door.

Oddly, we've never spoken of it since. We just live in the pretend world of denial. But that experience left me with deep feelings of rejection. I wanted her to see me, to validate my experience, but the intimacy never came.

God has recently revealed a deeper meaning for intimacy that explains why it's been tricky for me. When you say the word *intimacy* it can easily be changed to into–me–see. And I believe it's the cry of a woman's heart—*see me, know me, and love me anyway.*

I want others to know my coffee order. I want them to know where I prefer to sit in the movie theater. I want others to know that I can't drive by a McDonald's without getting a Diet Coke. Even more, I want someone to know the woundings of my heart, the pain of my past, and the challenges of my today. And when they do, it whispers into my heart, *You're worth knowing.*

I know this seems lofty. This is a tall order. It requires time. It requires listening. It requires watching. It requires putting down the electronic device long enough to connect. This level of knowing is a commitment. It's intimate knowledge. And it requires vulnerability.

I can recall times I've put myself out there, took a chance, and ended up rejected. I allowed people in and they didn't like what they saw. It left me thinking I wasn't good enough, or I was too high-maintenance, or even that I wasn't likeable. I wondered if they thought I wasn't skinny enough, or pretty enough, or funny enough to be friends with them—questions that came from my wounded heart. Continuing to be vulnerable in a world that's mean is a risky adventure. But it's the only way we'll ever create intimacy.

I had to learn to manage my expectations though. Intimate relationships take time, prayer, and grace. I've asked God to untangle the knots of insecurity in my marriage so I can enjoy time alone with my husband. And he is doing it. I've asked him for a group of women to challenge me, pray for me, and celebrate me, and he has blessed me with amazing friends. And someday God will open the door for me to finish that conversation with my mom.

But most of all, I've asked God to fill that space in me that longs to be seen. Because it's out of that fullness I can be confident enough in myself to be vulnerable and have intimacy in all of my relationships.

~ Karen

His Anchor

God judges persons differently than humans do. Men and women look at the face; God looks into the heart. (1 Sam. 16:7)

> He's not impressed with horsepower;
> the size of our muscles means little to him. (Ps. 147:10)

> The heart is hopelessly dark and deceitful,
> a puzzle that no one can figure out.
> But I, God, search the heart
> and examine the mind.
> I get to the heart of the human.
> I get to the root of things.
> I treat them as they really are,
> not as they pretend to be. (Jer. 17:9–10)

Jesus said to them, "You are the ones who make yourselves look right in other people's sight, but God knows your hearts. For the things that are considered of great value by people are worth nothing in God's sight." (Luke 16:15 GNT)

You made all the delicate, inner parts of my body and knit them together in my mother's womb. Thank you for making me so wonderfully complex! It is amazing to think about. Your workmanship is marvelous—and how well I know it. You were there while I was being formed in utter seclusion! You saw me before I was born and scheduled each day of my life before I began to breathe. Every day was recorded in your book! (Ps. 139:13–16 TLB)

───── Your Untangling Prayer ─────

Father, I am a tangled mess. I'm struggling to feel like I matter. There are so many messages echoing in my mind that reinforce the belief that I'm not good enough. They've left me overwhelmed with feelings of worthlessness.

I know your Word clearly tells me of my immeasurable value, but I can't seem to accept that it's true. Would you deposit that truth deep in my heart?

I'm tired of feeling unimportant. I'm tired of feeling like I'll never measure up. I'm tired of working so hard for approval and never getting it. My heart is weary, and I am desperate for the rest only you can provide.

The world has had me on the performance treadmill, making me work to prove my worth. I'm trying so hard to find significance in all the wrong places. And I realize now that I will never find my worth apart from you.

Would you please untangle me? I know you are the only One who can.

In the name of Jesus. Amen.

───── Loosening the Knot Questions ─────

1. In all the areas we can struggle as women, what area is the trickiest for you? Ask God to show you why, and journal about it.

2. How has your struggle with self-worth affected your relationships?

3. What event or season in life has tangled you the most? Where was God in it then? Where is he in it today?

4. What is the Holy Spirit speaking to you right now?

4

It Takes Two to *Tangle*

As I sit down to write this chapter, I'm a little miffed at my man. The dude knows how to push my buttons, and sometimes I think he enjoys it.

Whether it's innate or a conscious decision, my husband, Wayne, often corrects me and the kids when we say something inaccurate. Ugh. Heaven forbid I use the wrong tense or butcher a phrase, because if I do he'll let me know. When I'm joking around with the kids, trying to convince them that America has fifty-five states instead of fifty, he's quick to call my bluff. If my answer to his question doesn't sound right, he'll grab his phone and search the internet to solve his curiosity. It's super annoying.

His compulsive correction habit even translates to the written word, but this one usually works in our favor. There are times his grammatical knowledge comes in handy, like when I need an editor's eye or the kids need their homework proofed. He is crazy talented at catching errors.

My husband is also very smart. Our kids can ask the most random questions about something even more random, and he almost always knows the answers. From math equations to ancient China to black holes to political agendas to sports trivia, few things stump him. It's actually pretty amazing. I often call him "Cliff Clavin," the fictional *Cheers* character played by John Ratzenberger, who had a knack of knowing a little bit about a lot of things. Wayne is the same way. He retains almost everything he's heard, read, or experienced. I'm usually in awe of how packed full of information his brain is. But this morning, I most certainly was not.

As I was buttering a bagel, he started reading an article I'd written. It was an unsolicited read, of course. And rather than comment on how brilliant I was or how much the story touched his heart, he said, "This sentence is missing a period." Tangle.

My family—especially my husband—knows that I have a zero-tolerance policy on critical and rude comments before my morning coffee. I'm not the most gracious person in the morning. But as much as I would've liked to blame my frustration on not being fully caffeinated, I couldn't. His correction tightened a knot that was already twisted around my self-esteem, and it said, *You're not a good enough writer. You should have caught that yourself.*

Wouldn't you agree that marriage can be a huge trigger for our *not good enough* struggle? Since we spend so much time with our spouses, opportunities to offend one another abound. He might say something that makes me feel like a lousy wife, or I might make him feel like a bad provider. There are times we intentionally pick at each other, but most of the time our words and actions aren't intended to hurt. They're just taken the wrong way.

Sometimes when we're frustrated, we take it out on each other because it feels safe. I know Wayne won't walk out on me if I'm a little cranky, or if I make a bigger deal out of something than I should. I'm important to him, and his heart is for me. I know things about my man that no one else does, and he has dirt on me too. Sometimes we use that information as a weapon against each other. But there's deep validation in knowing I am worth the fight, and he won't quit on our marriage regardless of how hard it gets.

It's no secret there are huge differences in how men and women communicate. It can make understanding each other difficult and hurting each other's feelings easy. And that might be the understatement of the year. But a key to making marriage work is being able to find a way to share your heart in a way the other can understand. Being that vulnerable can seem risky to your wounded self-esteem, but it's a powerful way to build trust and confidence in your husband. Sometimes they need us to give them that opportunity again.

Wayne has seen my ugly cry, the one where snot and mascara have a party on my face, and has stupidly commented on it. That one didn't end well. And I've said things to emasculate him—sometimes on purpose. And knowing each other's insecurities, there have been times we've deliberately poked them.

I'm not trying to be Debbie Downer when it comes to marriage. I absolutely love being married to Wayne. There are countless great things about my man, like how we understand the meaning behind each other's facial expressions without speaking a word. Or how, when the kids send me to the brink of insanity, he knows how to talk me off the ledge. I love the family we've made together and the memories that are too risqué to share. I appreciate how when I turn into a psycho drama queen, he remains steady and calm. Plus, he's hot.

Marriage is an adventure in vulnerability. As much as we want our husbands to know the real us and see right into our soul, it's scary to let them in. There are fragile places inside where we've been deeply hurt before—places where we feel we'll never measure up. Opening our black and blue hearts to intimacy means taking that risk again, but that's what marriage is all about.

Intimacy and Insecurity

Mark 10:8 tells us intimacy in marriage is God's design. He says, "he and his wife are united so that they are no longer two, but one" (TLB). This verse means the lines that individually define me and Wayne—that define you and your husband—become blurred when you get married. They fade, and a new border that now surrounds you as a couple becomes more distinct. Two become one and together you become powerful for the kingdom (Matt. 18:19), and the Enemy hates it. And so he does all he can to make those individual lines hard to erase, triggering our insecurity and rubbing our self-esteem raw in the process.

When There Is Disunity between Husband and Wife

When a man and woman marry, it means life is shared—hopes, dreams, struggles, victories, dessert, and the like. God wants us to do life together. As husband and wife, we become each other's cheerleader. We support and offer help when needed. And we look for ways to encourage and affirm each other every day.

So when there is disunity in that relationship, for whatever reason, our self-esteem is affected. In those seasons where Wayne and I aren't getting along, feelings of insecurity surface, making me wonder if I'm even worth his effort. I start operating in self-protection mode, and that fear causes me to withdraw even more. This time, I'm sure I've pushed him too far.

My self-confidence plummets and I spiral into self-condemnation. And at the end of the day I want him to wrap his arms around me and say everything will be okay, but I'm scared he'll reject me if I ask. So I don't.

Conflict is a normal part of any relationship. And when we're already struggling to feel worthy as a wife, disunity can be devastating.

When We Put Our Husbands on the Throne

As women, we long to feel secure and cared for. We want the answer to the question "Am I worth the fight?" to be a resounding "Yes!" While past wounds might make it harder to let down our guard and trust our men, at the core we want to be seen. We want to feel protected. And when our husbands don't fight for us or forgive the mistakes we've made, the message of *not worth it* settles in.

Other times, we put our men on the throne and work to impress them. We often let our husband's opinion of us determine how we feel about ourselves. When they are critical of how we handled a situation we feel foolish. We worry what they'll think of dinner, especially since we're not a culinary genius. When they don't notice the results from our workout we lose self-confidence. And when they do notice or comment favorably we feel on top of the world.

While our husbands are called to be the head of our homes, they are not called to be our saviors. That position has already been filled by Jesus himself. And when we place too much emphasis on their opinion of us, we make them our God.

When We Let the State of Our Marriage Affect Our Self-Confidence

As long as we feel adored by our men, we're sure we can tackle the world. When we're getting along with our husbands, our outlook on life is bright. And after a night of sweet intimacy together, there's a spring in our step. We are loving life.

Few things can boost my self-confidence like a deep connection with my husband. You too? That good feeling seeps into every area of life, doesn't it? We take more pride in our appearance because our man thinks we're one hot mama. We feel more positive, alive, focused, and able to tackle our day.

But when marriage gets crunchy, our self-confidence gets tangled. It's destabilizing. We worry if—how—things will work out. Fear creeps in and whispers, *This time he's leaving*. Guilt says, *You did it again*. And shame says, *You're not worth the trouble*. Our frame of mind changes from one of confidence to one of insecurity, and we withdraw. We replay the fight in our minds over and over and over again . . . because that's what women do.

When we allow people and situations to influence how we feel about ourselves, our self-worth will never be secure. Our self-confidence will change when the wind does. That's why we have Jesus. He is the only voice we should let speak into our insecure hearts, because in his eyes our significance never changes.

～ ⌁ ～

Growing up, I never thought about marriage much. Why would anyone spend time dreaming of the white picket fence and 2.5 kids when they feel completely unworthy of that kind of love? I knew I was broken. I believed I was worthless. After all, my abuser had told me so, and my little four-year-old heart still accepted it as truth, no matter how much time had passed. And with a string of broken relationships and heartaches behind me, I was certain of it.

My first marriage failed. Yep, that was a great self-esteem booster. Even as I was walking down the aisle, there were a million red flags waving in my face, warning me to run away. But because I thought this was my only chance at love, I ignored them all. I walked into that marriage hoping it would heal my wounded, bruised heart. It didn't. I wanted it to fix me. It couldn't. Two years later I limped out, dragging my confidence behind me. We divorced, and I adopted the title of *failure*.

It was the perfect addition to all the other labels I wore—labels like *unlovable*, *ugly*, *unacceptable*, *disappointing*—the ones that reminded me I was worthless. The days that followed were very dark days. Rather than run to Jesus, I asked the world to make me feel better. I just wanted to be loved. I wanted someone to rescue me. I craved approval. And then I met the man who would become my second husband. Baggage always attracts baggage. You can take that to the bank.

I'm not sure you could put two more broken people together. Messy, messy, messy. We had quite a résumé between us—abuse, addiction, anger, unforgiveness, trust issues, control tendencies, and a suitcase full of insecurities. It was a match made in heaven. And because we thought marriage would solve all our problems, we decided to forgo premarital counseling and jump in feetfirst. Within the first few months, we were in intensive counseling.

We had no clue just how wounded we were. The Enemy is brilliant at covering our eyes from the truth, but we couldn't miss the downward spiral of our marriage. My issues were butting up against his issues, his baggage was triggering my baggage, and we kept hurting each other. I felt worthless as a spouse, and lived in fear that divorce number two was right around the corner. Because I was the common denominator in both marriages, I wondered, *What is wrong with me?*

As much as I wanted to duck and run—and believe me, we both did—I held on. There were some temporary fixes and Band-Aid seasons, but in those first few years I never felt secure in my marriage. I worried he was going to walk away, just like my first husband did. And then we got pregnant with a baby boy. Fourteen months after he was born, we welcomed our little girl. I prayed these babies would be a remedy, but it wasn't that simple. We needed more than two plump little cherubs to fix our marriage. We needed divine intervention.

It's been fifteen years of watching God continue untangling the knots of insecurity that marriage can trigger. My husband has become a confident leader in our home, and I feel loved and valued by my man. We're nicer to each other, quicker to forgive. Our marriage isn't perfect. It still pokes those *not good enough* feelings, but it's also healing some of them. If you're waiting and praying for a miracle in your own marriage, don't give up. Your prayers and cries reach the heavens, and you are worthy of saving. "That is why I wait expectantly, trusting God to help, for he has promised" (Ps. 130:5 TLB). Hang in there.

False Expectations

I think we'd all agree that marriage isn't a cakewalk. For some of us, that's a gross understatement. My dad has always said that marriage is an unnatural act. We each bring different life experiences, different insecurities, different ideas, and different hopes into the relationship. Weave in our gender issues and unique personalities, and it gets . . . ahem . . . interesting. Twist in the unrealistic expectations the world places on wives (and husbands), and we become a tangled mess—and are set up for failure.

The Sexually Assertive Wife

If you ask any man what he wants from his wife, knowing she desires him sexually will be at the top of the list. Men want to be wanted. They want to feel desired by their wives. It's a normal longing that makes a man, well, a man. But in this area, it can be tricky for a woman to be what her husband needs.

Some of us have been victims of sexual abuse, making intimacy difficult. Abuse leaves us feeling worthless, dirty, and tarnished. We struggle to trust our husbands with this part of ourselves, because it feels too risky—even when they're the good guys.

The abuse I experienced as a child has robbed me and my husband of being able to fully enjoy sexual intimacy. I love to be with him, but I'm rarely the initiator. If I were able to be more sexually assertive, it would speak volumes into my man's self-esteem. But it's tricky. Sometimes I feel guilt and shame for not being more of what I know he'd like. I wonder if I'm letting him down, failing at being a wife. But God has been untangling this knot, and I'm hopeful for continued healing. If you've been a victim of sexual abuse, please ask for help. Your church should have resources and counselors they can recommend. Without professional help and divine intervention, the chances of this tangle unraveling on its own are slim to none.

The media doesn't help us feel good about our sexuality either. We compare our libido to those characters on our favorite shows or movies. They promote a standard that's truly ridiculous, but one many of us are buying into. So often, Hollywood portrays women as do-it-anywhere, want-it-all-the-time, rip-their-clothes-off sex machines. In these shows, they might be sleep-deprived surgeons, but they need to get busy in the supply closet several times a day. They're moms with screaming kids and dirty dishes all over the kitchen, but when their man comes home it's party time. Really?

And as we watch these shows, we compare our bedroom experiences with theirs, our passion with theirs, and our frequency of sex with theirs. We're left feeling guilty, convinced we're not passionate enough in the bedroom and shamed because we don't have the desire to be.

We read novels that entice us into fantasyland, often with hot fictional men who enjoy being a bit deviant. Somehow, the author makes handcuffing or blindfolding a tender experience. They make us want to spice things up in the bedroom, but rather than be in the moment with our husbands we're replaying those steamy scenes from the book in our imagination. Some might argue it's sexual assertiveness, but I consider it fifty shades of false intimacy. And when we can't get reality and fantasy to mirror each other between the sheets, we feel a huge letdown. We consider ourselves dysfunctional. Our attempts to be a sexual dynamo have failed, and we go back to the status quo. We grab our soft porn novels and disappear into the pages where we feel *good enough* too. We long for something that's not real, and we feel cheated.

Sexual intimacy between a husband and wife is beautiful. It's God's design. But we're bombarded with messages that pervert it and make us feel guilty for seeing it that way. I'm sick of it.

We're not only to be kinky and insatiable, but also to have the perfect bedroom body. So we try. We strive for the right lighting and shading. We find the perfect position to hide flaws in our figure. Am I speaking anyone's language? We dress up in slutty outfits to set the mood, and drink alcohol to relax us so we're less inhibited. But I wonder, do these tactics make you feel more beautiful? More desirable? More valuable?

Now please hear my heart on this. Sometimes a girl's gotta do what a girl's gotta do. There is nothing wrong with making some adjustments to feel more confident. I'm not sitting in judgment, because the Lord knows I can identify with some of the things on this list. But let me ask you a question: If you recognize yourself in that list, are you trying to compensate for your *not good enough* feelings? Do you think you're only desirable *if* and *when*? If so, it might be a tangle to ask God to unknot.

The Forever Young Wife

I was looking in my magnifying mirror, the one that uncovers every flaw, trying to pluck that pesky whisker from my chin. Oh, and it's white. Awesome. What's up with these rogue hairs anyway? I used to ask my husband to hunt it down, but I've learned to pluck on my own. I assumed that if I was grossed out by his ear hair, my chin whisker didn't help my cause.

As I was trying to find the right angle, I noticed three Grand Canyon–deep wrinkles above my top lip. I screamed in horror. *Are you kidding me? How many people have noticed and kept their mouths shut?* I was so self-conscious.

That same day, I called the spa for a facial. I meant business. I bought a package of microdermabrasion sessions and other services that promised to erase the signs of age, and went religiously each week. After a few months, I asked my husband if he noticed anything different about my face and he froze in fear. Poor guy. Few things unravel a man more than having to answer a question like that. I could see panic in his eyes as he listed off a few go-to answers, none of which were right.

When I told him I was plagued with rogue hairs and facial crevasses and shared the treatments I'd subjected myself to, he shook his head. "Carey, I never saw a problem to begin with. You look beautiful to me no matter what. I love growing old with you."

In his mind, my wrinkled upper lip and annoying chin hair had nothing to do with my beauty. He saw my heart. The reason I struggle with it all is because I often tie my worth to my youth.

As I look at my handsome, balding, wrinkled, gray-haired man, I wonder why I think it is acceptable for him to age but not me. Why am I expected to look ten years younger? Why are men considered distinguished while women are old biddies? Why should my skin be flawless, my figure flattering, and my hair full? Why are we expected to stay forever young? This mindset keeps us from loving our aging bodies.

As wives, we want to look good for our husbands. We attend fitness classes to tighten our tush, get our hair colored to hide the gray, and put together outfits to look cute. We invest in antiaging skin products to turn back the clock, inject Botox in our face to hide wrinkles, and go through medical procedures to restore this or reduce that. And when our husband tells us we're beautiful no matter what, we don't receive it.

This tangle is one we usually weave ourselves. In our insecurity, we don't trust that our husband could actually find our aging body attractive. But there's something sweet about growing old together.

My husband tells me I'm more attractive now than when we first met, and I feel the same way about him. Beauty is indeed in the eye of the beholder.

Somewhere along the line, we've bought into the lie that getting older means we're no longer attractive. It feeds our insecurities, and we go to extreme measures to look years younger than we are. It makes sense though. We see older men with younger women on their arm and panic it might happen in our own marriage. Our husbands probably work with women who are youthful and perky, and we can't help but wonder if our men see us as a disappointment. Women in Hollywood look remarkable for their age. (I would too with a personal trainer, personal chef, personal surgeons, and very deep pockets to pay for it all.)

If we decide our worth is dependent on defying the aging process, we will never feel good about ourselves—because it's a battle we can never win.

The Superwife

In the 1980s, a fragrance commercial hit the airways that boasted "This is the eight-hour perfume for the twenty-four-hour woman." You may remember the product, Enjoli. The ad campaign was brilliant because it set the expectation that we are to be a superwoman of sorts. From cooking to carpooling, homework to housework, bills to baking, loving to laundry, and jobs to juggling everyone's schedules, women are expected to be everything for the family. Nothing can compete with our super powers.

But so much guilt is connected to this expectation. If we work outside the home, we're concerned with the amount of time we're away from our duties at home. If we are at home with the kids, we feel bad we're not helping pay the bills. So we overcompensate by becoming a superwife. Unless we do it all, we're not doing enough. And we're exhausted.

Then we tangle ourselves even more by reading about the Proverbs 31 woman, because apparently she can do it all. See for yourself:

> A good woman is hard to find,
> and worth far more than diamonds.
> Her husband trusts her without reserve,
> and never has reason to regret it.
> Never spiteful, she treats him generously
> all her life long.
> She shops around for the best yarns and cottons,
> and enjoys knitting and sewing.
> She's like a trading ship that sails to faraway places
> and brings back exotic surprises.
> She's up before dawn, preparing breakfast
> for her family and organizing her day.
> She looks over a field and buys it,
> then, with money she's put aside, plants a garden.
> First thing in the morning, she dresses for work,
> rolls up her sleeves, eager to get started.
> She senses the worth of her work,
> is in no hurry to call it quits for the day.
> She's skilled in the crafts of home and hearth,
> diligent in homemaking.
> She's quick to assist anyone in need,
> reaches out to help the poor.
> She doesn't worry about her family when it snows;
> their winter clothes are all mended and ready to wear.
> She makes her own clothing,
> and dresses in colorful linens and silks.
> Her husband is greatly respected
> when he deliberates with the city fathers.
> She designs gowns and sells them,
> brings the sweaters she knits to the dress shops.
> Her clothes are well-made and elegant,
> and she always faces tomorrow with a smile.

When she speaks she has something worthwhile to say,
    and she always says it kindly.
She keeps an eye on everyone in her household,
    and keeps them all busy and productive.
Her children respect and bless her;
    her husband joins in with words of praise:
"Many women have done wonderful things,
    but you've outclassed them all!"
Charm can mislead and beauty soon fades.
    The woman to be admired and praised
    is the woman who lives in the Fear-of-God.
Give her everything she deserves!
    Festoon her life with praises! (vv. 10–31)

Stick a fork in me—I'm done. These verses tangle me up because I struggle to find myself anywhere in them. Without a doubt, this woman should be admired and praised. She's the whole enchilada, while I sometimes feel like the crusty refried beans stuck to the plate.

What we fail to realize is that this woman had servants to help her. She didn't accomplish all this on her own. And this description of her awesomeness spans a lifetime of accomplishments—not one week. But regardless, we use this passage of Scripture as a measuring stick of how we're doing. We determine our worth by how we compare to her. And too often we're left holding the short end of the stick. That was never God's intent.

I know some women who make the superwife role look so easy. They don't get frazzled by insane to-do lists. Work-crazy husbands don't bother them. They're gracious to take on more chores. And they'll tell me, "I appreciate the opportunity to serve my husband and kids, because I consider them my mission field." Bleh. I think I just threw up in my mouth a little.

I love my family too. But I am a mere mortal. And I'm tired of feeling worthless because of it.

Truth is, I can be this super kind of wife and mom. I love to bless my family—for a while anyway. But when they start expecting me to do it all and all the time, it gets old quick. And then I lose it on someone, which never ends well. I go from being a superwoman to a super loser, feeling like the worst wife and mom on the planet.

Most of the time, I get tangled up in this one all by myself. I want a warm meal on the dinner table. I want an uncluttered home and clean laundry. I want to manage schedules seamlessly. I want the best for my family. But because of my human-sized limitations, I can't always make that happen. And I'm learning that it's okay. My human condition isn't a deficit.

God is graciously untangling my unrealistic expectation of being a superwife and supermom. Instead of it triggering those *not good enough* feelings, I'm learning to accept that my role is to be my family's support, not their savior.

───

But God does have realistic expectations for husbands and wives. His Word is clear about how we should care for one another. And reading what God has to say about our different roles in marriage makes me glad I'm a woman.

Here's a short list of how God expects men to treat their wives:

Be fair and don't take advantage of her (Col. 3:19).

Treat her with respect (1 Pet. 3:7).

Lead the marriage and family (Eph. 5:22–24).

Love her as you love yourself (Eph. 5:33).

Just like Jesus loved the church, love her with an attitude of giving and not getting (Eph. 5:25).

Be committed to her (1 Tim. 3:35).

View sexual intimacy as important for both of you instead of a place to make selfish demands (1 Cor. 7:2–6).

Be united with her instead of your parents (Matt. 19:5).

Here's how God expects wives to treat their husbands:

Respect and honor him (Eph. 5:33).

Understand and support him in ways that show your support for Christ (Eph. 5:22).

Place yourself under his authority in God-honoring ways (Col. 3:18).

I love having the shorter list. By the way, that last point sure gets a bad rap. The world conditions us to see surrendering to our husbands as becoming a doormat. It suggests we'll open ourselves to abuse and will eventually lose our voice. But let me ask you a question: Would God dictate a mandate designed to make his daughters feel worthless? No way. As a matter of fact, when we decide to love our husbands as God intended, the unexpected happens.

In 2011, God challenged me to do the impossible. He asked me to step out of the leadership role in my marriage—a position I'd held since day one. I knew that unless I did, my husband would never have the confidence to step forward. But it was a layered request.

Leading comes easily to me. It's how I'm wired, and it's also served as a defense mechanism designed to keep me safe. A counselor once told me it's a byproduct of the abuse I suffered as a child. Yep. And my husband grew up with a strong mom ruling the roost, so a female-dominated home was familiar. That was a dangerous combination.

But little by little, I began giving up control. It was frustrating to watch him struggle making decisions, ones I could have made in a split second. Instead of reminding him to do things, I kept my mouth shut and let him figure it out. I stopped nagging. I used my words to encourage and validate instead. At times, I had to turn my back as the words left my mouth—my face would have shown my disbelief. I let him make mistakes without *I-told-you-sos*. And while I'd been comfortable wearing the pants in the marriage, deep down I resented him for it.

I wanted Wayne to cherish me. I wanted him to restore what my abuser took away. I wanted him to be strong and decisive, having a backbone to fight for his woman. I needed him to be passionately in love with me and sweep me off my feet. At the core, I wanted him to save me because nobody ever had. And since these things hadn't happened, the Enemy's voice whispered, *You don't deserve a man like that.* But God had different plans.

As I gave up control, things shifted. Wayne's confidence grew by leaps and bounds. He began to treat me better, complimenting me and bringing gifts home. *I really liked this.* He took initiative to plan date nights. When others hurt my feelings, he'd get angry on my behalf. *I liked this even better.* He started taking more responsibility with the kids and at home, often without me asking.

And you know what happened? His self-worth untangled because he felt respected, and my self-worth untangled because I felt like I mattered. It was a win-win all the way around. And God used our marriage to do it. When we aligned ourselves with God's plan, the insecurities that knotted up our self-esteem loosened.

The relationship between husband and wife is strategic. 1 Corinthians 11:11 says, "But remember that in God's plan men and women need each other" (TLB). God uses marriage to reveal our tangles and untie the *not good enough* lies attached to them. No other earthly relationship is set up with that kind of power. But rather than embrace it, the world mocks it.

It suggests marriage will take from your life rather than add to it. We hear phrases like, "If marriage isn't a prison, why do they call it wedlock?" and "Wedding rings: the world's smallest handcuffs." When did we liken marriage to jail? Celebrities even chime in:

"Marriage is a great institution, but I'm not ready for an institution."[1] (Mae West)

"I don't know anything about sex. I've always been married."[2] (Zsa Zsa Gabor)

"The surest way to be alone is to get married."[3] (Gloria Steinem)

While these comments may be funny, marriage continues to take a beating. Groups are redefining it. Courts are reworking it. People are refusing it.

When we put the world at the center of our marriage, that mindset will filter into our self-worth. Marriage will morph from divine to common, and our insecurities will run rampant because we'll try to untangle our own knots. But when we put God at the center, everything changes. We will love better, forgive faster, and give grace easier—and God will use it all to untangle our brokenness.

Her Tangle: A Story from Sarah

Tears are streaming down my face, and a popular song with the lyrics "I need a miracle" is playing on the radio as I leave the surgeon's office. It will take a few hours of more tears and prayer to realize I don't need a miracle. I *want* one. What I need, I already have.

As I digest the news, I wrestle with a lie—the one I've wrestled with for years—that says because I am single, I won't have the provision I need. Truth is, I'll need lots of help to recover. Three to six months is a long time to ask friends to help. And the finances will be interesting. I'm not sure how all my ends will meet.

But more than help and provision for this journey, what I really want is intimacy. I don't want to be walking this alone as a single woman. I want a husband to hold my hand as I'm wheeled into surgery. I want to wake to his smile. And while I've had a few opportunities to marry, each time I knew it wasn't God's best for me. It's times like these the Enemy's voice speaks loud though, reminding me of missed opportunities. I hate the lies he whispers in my ears.

My desire for a miracle is rooted in these lies. Being single can be just as powerful a trigger in the hands of the Enemy as being married. One of my biggest tangles has been struggling to believe with my whole being that the Lord will provide for *all* of my needs—even my need for the kind of intimacy marriage offers.

Since I was a little girl, my dream has been to be a wife and mom. While I've never been either, I still hope for both. Yet to live fully today rather than hoping for tomorrow can be challenging. I've had to learn the difference between a *need* and a *want* regarding marriage.

I've dated men who wanted to marry me and men I've wanted to marry. None of these relationships moved toward marriage until I was in my mid-thirties. I reconnected with a man I'd dated seven years earlier, and after a few months our relationship took off.

I remember the moment I knew he was the one. It was a moment I'll never forget. But within a few weeks, he shared a dark secret—he told me about his addiction to pornography. It hit me like a ton of bricks.

He said he had been in counseling for years, trying to break it off. Later that summer I started going to counseling sessions with him. He'd been working with this man for years, but the addiction kept holding on. At the same time, we began attending a premarital class at my church. I kept wondering, *Is this God's best for me?*

Through the counseling, I began to see the wall between us, one that was blocking emotional intimacy. I thought it would dissolve as we worked through the issues, but it didn't. I poured prayer over what to do, telling God that I wanted what he wanted for me. And then this man came over for "the talk."

While we both decided to stick it out and work through the issues, something didn't feel right. And a few days later, the truth came out. He'd decided the pornography addiction was easier than working on intimacy with me. As he walked out the door, I heard God say, *Don't run after him. Turn to me.* I stayed in bed most of the next few days, devastated that the relationship had ended. God was so comforting to me during that time. Even though my heart longed for intimacy, battling that kind of addiction would have sucked the life out of me. I realized how the Lord had brought me into a closer relationship with him so he could fulfill my need for intimacy.

I've seen several friends struggle in marriages where the husband was addicted to pornography. Not only does the Enemy trigger all of the insecurities in these women, but he threatens the marriage itself. God saved me from that.

I've been a Christ-follower for over half my life. Being single, I've had time to dig into God's Word. The discipline I've learned through Bible studies and discipleship training has given me a great foundation and hunger for studying the Word daily. And that's created an atmosphere where I could hear the Lord and grow in my relationship with him.

Now I understand that whatever my circumstances, whether married or single, it's my relationship with Jesus that provides the intimacy my heart longs for. I'm worth his time and his effort, and he would never choose anything else over me.

Although God has untangled most of my insecurities about being single, I continue to wrestle with lies surrounding the Lord's provision. This latest journey with my health has been a six-year struggle. I've been learning how to separate *needs* from *wants*, and relying on the Lord's provision in ways I would have never known otherwise.

Perhaps one day, I will have an earthly husband—a *want* supplied by the Lord. But until then, I have a heavenly one, and he promises to meet all my needs.

~ Sarah

His Anchor

God said, "It's not good for the Man to be alone; I'll make him a helper, a companion." (Gen. 2:18)

House and riches are the inheritance from fathers, but a wise, understanding, and prudent wife is from the Lord. (Prov. 19:14 AMP)

A capable, intelligent, and virtuous woman—who is he who can find her? She is far more precious than jewels and her value is far above rubies or pearls. (Prov. 31:10 AMP)

Avoid the passions of youth, and strive for righteousness, faith, love, and peace, together with those who with a pure heart call out to the Lord for help. (2 Tim. 2:22 GNT)

Love is very patient and kind, never jealous or envious, never boastful or proud, never haughty or selfish or rude. Love does not demand its own way. It is not irritable or touchy. It does not hold grudges and will hardly even notice when others do it wrong. It is never glad about injustice, but rejoices whenever truth wins out. If you love someone, you will be loyal to him no matter what the cost. You will always believe in him, always expect the best of him, and always stand your ground in defending him. (1 Cor. 13:4–7 TLB)

Your Untangling Prayer

Father, thank you for creating marriage. I know it's designed to be a safe place to grow and heal, but sometimes it's scary to be vulnerable. Would you help me embrace all that marriage should be?

Thank you for blessing me with my husband. Help me be the kind of wife that loves him no matter what. Give him a heart for me too. And let us see each other as partners rather than saviors.

Lord, would you untangle my self-esteem from all the places I've tied it in my marriage? I don't want to find my worth in anything but you. Please give me a healthy perspective on what marriage is and what it is not. Remind me that my husband isn't my knight in shining armor. You are.

And Lord, give me the ability to stand firm in my commitment when I want to walk away. Give me the spiritual eyes to see the bigger picture, and to trust you are working through our struggles. Tame the control freak inside me so it doesn't bleed into my marriage.

I pray all this in the sweet name of Jesus. Amen.

───ᶜ Loosening the Knot Questions ᵔ───

1. Where do your insecurities show up the most in your marriage? Why?

2. How would your husband say you tangle his self-esteem? What do you need God to change in you?

3. What did your parents' marriage look like? How is yours similar? Different? Can you identify where your insecurities came from?

4. What is the Holy Spirit speaking to you right now?

Tangled Up in Our Kids

"Mom, I can't take it anymore."

I stood up, closed the refrigerator door, and turned to see my then-third-grade son standing behind me. He was crying.

"What's happened, Sam?"

He began to unpack his struggle of the past three years—events he'd kept hidden from me and my husband. As I sat and listened, tears rolled quietly down my cheeks. But inside I was screaming. How could this have happened right under my nose? Wasn't I supposed to protect my children? Guilt sucker-punched me in the gut and said, *You're a horrible mom.*

Sam shared how a boy in class had been bullying him. And it hadn't just been that school year, but the better part of three years. Although the offender was in my son's grade, he was taller and outweighed him by a good fifteen pounds. Sam had been kicked, chased, hit, pinched, taunted, and threatened with his life if he told me or anyone else about it. Because he was afraid this kid would make good on his threat, Sam had kept silent about the situation. Until now.

I'd heard this boy's name before. I knew he bothered my son from time to time, and I had counseled him through a few situations. But I didn't realize it had crossed the line from mean kid to bully. As a mom, shouldn't I have seen the shift? How did I miss that?

All of the normal questions came up, like, "Have you told your teacher? The principal? Did you fight back or stand up for yourself?" He had talked to them several times, but I hadn't received any phone call from the school. Their advice was to let it go, or stay away from him, or work it out himself. Sam didn't stand up for himself because he'd been taught to turn the other cheek, a motto we've since drastically revised. My son felt abandoned, like he wasn't worth fighting for.

We had noticed little changes in Sam's schoolwork, but nothing drastic. His handwriting was sloppy and he struggled in math, previously his strongest subject. He stopped doing homework, telling us he had none. His A grades were dropping to Bs. And at parent-teacher conferences, they blamed the changes on anything from rushing through his work to learning harder math concepts.

There were changes in him too, but they were subtle and gradual and, we assumed, normal. Sam seemed angrier and had a quick temper. His eating and sleeping habits shifted. He struggled socially and had lost self-confidence. We asked doctors and therapists if these changes were worrisome, and they assured us he was normal and things would be okay. Even as I type this out, I feel guilt wash over me. Why didn't I see the situation more clearly?

We immediately pulled him from the neighborhood school, enrolled him in a Christian private school, and began counseling with a woman I'm certain was appointed for a time such as this. It was during therapy that most of the details surrounding the bullying emerged. Hearing about the evil my son endured overwhelmed me and awoke the mama-bear inside. I was furious, but underneath was always crushing guilt. I'm not sure I've ever cried as much as I did through those months. And then the unimaginable happened.

While I was sitting in the school's pick-up line, the principal called and asked me to meet in her office. I walked in to find Sam sitting, head down. My heart started racing while trying to make sense of this meeting. Was there another bully situation? Did Sam lash out in anger? I sat down quietly as she said, "Carey, Sam told two teachers today that he wanted to commit suicide." My eyes met Sam's and I saw into his soul. And it scared me.

My guilt was the fuel behind finding the responsible party. I met with the previous school's teachers, principal, district administration, and even the school board itself. I even confronted the bully's mom. I was going to make this right—I had to. Someone was going to pay for my failure to save Sam from this horrible situation. But when my best efforts failed and I couldn't shift my guilt to another's blame, those self-condemning feelings flooded back.

A *good* mom would have understood the situation better. A *caring* mom would have known something was drastically different with her son. An *effective* mom would have nipped this in the bud. And a *worthless* mom would have done exactly what I did—nothing.

I was tangled in the lie that said it was my fault—that I'd failed my son. It said my best effort wasn't enough, and my kids deserved better. Few things can knock you to your knees more than knowing you've failed your children. I carried the blame alone until my husband said, "You're an amazing mom! None of us saw what was really going on, so stop beating yourself up." And his words shifted something in me.

God used them to rebuild my confidence. I was—I am—a good mom. I'm head over heels in love with my two nuggets, and love hanging out with them. Sweet mother, they make me laugh. We joke—a lot—and they dish it right back. Our family has a blast together. We hide behind doors and scare one another (not so fun with my fortysomething bladder). We wrestle and tickle fight all the time. There's nothing like hearing kids roll around with a good belly laugh. My husband and I rarely vacation without our kids because we enjoy them so much. And when we do travel alone, we miss them.

We have strict rules of engagement too. We treat each other with respect and kindness (most of the time, anyway). Each night, we pray as a family and my husband speaks a personalized blessing over each of them. We steward their hearts with great intention. Because we were told we couldn't have children, Wayne and I see Sam and Sara as the blessings they are.

So watching my son suffer because I didn't understand the gravity of the situation and intervene sooner tangled me. And to make matters worse, my best efforts to right the wrong got me nowhere. I was bloodied in the battle, and in the end I was left with a wounded son, a broken heart, and guilt the size of Texas on my shoulders.

It's been three years since Sam was bullied, and God has been faithfully restoring my son ever since. There have been layers of healing, but Sam is doing great today. I've forgiven myself for not understanding the seriousness of the situation. I know that God loves my son more than I could. And most of the time, I'm confident as a mom.

Guilt in parenting is a big deal. It's triggered when something we do or say hurts our kids, when our thoughts and actions don't align with our mom-of-the-year expectations, or when we fail to provide for or protect them. We think that being a mom means we can do it all, all the time, with a stellar attitude, no matter what. Um, right. No wonder we're set up to be guilt-ridden. We get tangled in an unrealistic standard—one no woman could ever meet.

I'm learning to cling to these words of freedom from Romans 3:23, "Yes, all have sinned; all fall short of God's glorious ideal" (TLB). *All* means everyone—you, me, Madonna, Mother Teresa, and anyone else who's ever breathed air. We aren't the only ones to fail our kids. We all mess up. There's relief in knowing we're all members of the same club. Grab your name tag on the way in. Welcome.

But it's what comes next in that passage that is life to me. Verse 24 says, "yet now God declares us 'not guilty' of offending him if we trust in Jesus Christ, who in his kindness freely takes away our sins." Guess what . . . I'm not guilty. And if you're a Christ-follower, neither are you. You're freed from the weight of guilt and the *I'm not a good mom* messages. When you fail, it's not held against you. Jesus promises to untangle you from guilt, freeing you up to be a purposeful mom rather than a perfect one.

And because God says I'm blameless, I'm not going to let my worth as a mom be determined by the world. Here's my top five list of things *not* to feel guilty about from this point forward.

5. Giving my kids formula when they were babies.

While many are able to successfully breastfeed their babies, I was not. And I've felt like a failure because of it. Standing in the checkout line, I was certain the proverbial spotlight was shining down on me saying, "Formula-buying loser-mom, right here!" Today, my kids are brilliant, well-adjusted, and active. And my Similac-feeding guilt is gone.

4. Bribing my kids with anything that might work.

Every now and then, it's *Let's Make a Deal* time in my house. My husband and I might be staring down a deadline, or feeling sick, or just needing a break from the insanity. Regardless, desperate times call for drastic measures. As long as it's legal and moral, bribing will be a guilt-free part of my toolbox.

3. Not being class mom or going on field trips.

Most of my friends are comfortable around groups of kids. Me? Not so much. When God was handing out little-people patience,

I obviously missed my portion. I was in line for "awesome hair," and by the time I got to the patience line, all the rations were gone. Truth is, kids love me. They want to touch and hug and hang on me. Just thinking about it makes me sweat—but at least it's a guiltless sweat.

2. Throwing away artwork.

I have several huge plastic tubs of artwork in my basement. Glitter nativity scenes, cotton ball mountain-scapes, paper towel roll statues, and countless other artistic masterpieces. I used to be a candidate for *Hoarders*, the television show where people struggle to get rid of odds and ends. But now I keep the cream of the crop and toss the rest. And if they notice their pinecone grizzly bear is gone, I'll blame it on Dad.

1. Saying "Because I said so!"

These words came out of my mouth just this morning, and my daughter gave me the look. You know, the one that says, *You're the worst mom ever!* But using the "Because I said so" line is a parenting perk. My mom used it, and her mom used it too. It's a generational blessing that comes in handy when I can't think of a better response to the question, "Why?" And I'm no longer letting my kids give me a guilt trip when I use it.

Guilt is just one strand of the motherhood tangle. There are plenty of others that make us feel just as inadequate. Motherhood knots our self-esteem because these little critters don't come with detailed instructions. Each new situation presents a new opportunity for us to mess up. Even if we've already figured it out with one child, all the rules change with the next.

We worry we're not punishing enough or the right way. We question the amount of quality time we spend with them. We wonder if we're pushing too hard or not enough. We're not sure when to say yes and when to stand firm with our no. There are seasons we feel one step behind the challenges facing our kids and we can't seem to get ahead. Motherhood is full of curve balls. And it leaves us feeling terribly inadequate.

Before we know it, the influence we have in the lives of our kids changes. Gone are the days where we had complete voting power in their decisions. They now listen more to their friends and other outside influences. It's a hard adjustment because we're used to being the center of their universe. Many of us found our identity in that, and now we're struggling to find how we fit into their lives. When my twelve-year-old got a haircut last week, I saw this play out perfectly.

His new 'do was awesome, and he went from looking homeless to handsome in a matter of twenty minutes. But even though the stylist had cut his hair exactly to his specifications, he hated it. I knew it the moment his eyes met mine. "Sam, you look really cool, dude!" I said. But all I heard was a series of sighs from the backseat, followed by, "You have to say that. You're my mom." My opinion didn't matter. And at home, the drama continued.

He jumped in the shower so he could fix his hair *his way*. When that didn't work, he pulled a stocking cap down over his head. To add to his dramatic performance, he put on a hoodie and closed the drawstring tight around his face. He huffed and puffed for the next thirty minutes, declaring everyone at school would make fun of him the next day. "Sam, don't worry," I said. "Your hair looks amazing!" But no matter how much I affirmed his cut, he was certain life as he knew it was over. I felt useless. Tweener Town ain't for the faint of heart, people.

The drive to school was uncomfortably quiet the next morning. It bothered me that my words couldn't help. I was begging God to close the mouth of any yahoo who might make a rude comment about Sam's hair. Ugh, I hate silent car rides. All day I stressed and prayed, and stressed and prayed more. I remembered with longing the days when a smile and hug fixed everything.

I sat in my car waiting for school to get out, anticipating tears. I was anxious and stirred up. Would I have the words to calm him? The door opened and he was all smiles. "Mom, everyone loved my haircut! They said it made me look cool." *Um, come again? Didn't I say that a million times yesterday?*

Truth is, it didn't matter what I said. He needed the A-OK from his buddies at school. And while he still loved me, he didn't need me the same way he used to. My role in his life had changed from a decider to a guider. I know my son loves and values me, but I'm no longer the center of his universe. While that's a normal and healthy response as my children grow up, it's hard. And the tangle happens when our sense of value is connected to our level of influence in the lives of our kids.

Sometimes we tie our worth to a child's success or failure. We put blood, sweat, and tears into raising kids and we want a return on our investment. We measure our success in parenting by their success in life. When they excel, it's because we're an excellent mom. But when they fall short, we obviously didn't do our job right. It's a jumbo-sized tangle that puts a whole lot of pressure on our kids. Here are a few examples.

Academic Achievements

I connected with a woman I hadn't seen in a while. She has a whole gaggle of kids and is one of the most overwhelmed moms I know. Raising so many kids has been a struggle, especially with a husband who travels. When I asked about her kids, she said, "They're great! Each one made the honor roll!"

Her beaming smile revealed the real message behind her statement. It said, "Don't you see that I'm a great mom?" I wanted to cup her face in my hands and tell her she was a wonderful mother whether her kids were on the honor roll or not. She tangled her performance as a mom to the grades her kids made in school.

And sometimes this can get nasty. When their kids are too tired, overwhelmed, or stressed, I've known moms to write papers or complete school projects. Other moms have argued with teachers over a bad grade. Some have turned a blind eye to plagiarism, giving their children permission to steal ideas and copy concepts for a good grade. And we've all seen moms who push their kids to the brink of a breakdown by heaping piles of unrealistic academic expectations on them.

Why do we do this? Because we think that if they fail, so do we. When we measure our achievements as a parent by the educational achievements of our kids, we'll compromise our better judgment to feel successful.

Social Calendars

Today, it seems we glorify a busy calendar. Our motto is "Busyness is next to godliness." Only it couldn't be further from the truth. What being busy does instead is give us a false sense of significance. And when our kid's schedule is packed, we consider it proof that we're raising a popular and talented prodigy.

As we try to schedule a coffee date with our friend, we listen as she rattles off her kid's crazy schedule—sports practices, piano lessons, student council meetings, parties, and other assorted appointments—and two things could happen.

First, we might feel inferior as a mom because our child's calendar is wide open. What have we done wrong? Rather than be as well-liked and gifted as her child, our kid is just . . . ordinary. Second, while she may faux-whine about her to-do list, her merit as a mom may feel affirmed. Be it good genes or supernatural abilities, in her mind she's done something right. Can you see the knot of insecurity in both responses?

Competitive Sports

Today's parents feel pressure for their kids to compete and excel in sports, and that expectation trickles down to the kids. We don't throw the football around for fun anymore, but because we're shaping the next Heisman Trophy winner. Instead of watching baseball for the love of the game, we consider each play a learning opportunity for our child.

In our minds, if they succeed in sports, we succeed in parenting. We want first stringers and MVPs, and allow their performance to reflect on us. I saw this play out when my daughter was in competitive gymnastics. A few moms walked around with an air of superiority because their daughters were among the highest scorers on the team. They would flood social media with their girl's beam and vault scores, and one mom even posted her ten-year-old daughter's washboard abs as her profile picture. Excuse me?

Listen, I'm all for sports and feeling pride in your child's accomplishments. But when it fills an empty place in our self-worth, it's not healthy. When we pour time and money and effort into making them winners because it satisfies something in us, we've been caught in a tangle. And when our children believe their worth is tied to their performance, they get caught in one too.

Awards and Recognition

It's no longer peer pressure that pushes our kids to outperform their classmates—it's unrealistic expectations from parents. We want our kids to achieve where we failed. We want them to be all we never could be.

I see this trying to manifest in my own parenting. Growing up, I always wanted to be a cheerleader. I tried out several times but never made it. I guess my jazz hands didn't impress. But now that I have a daughter in middle school, I find myself wanting to point her toward that sport. Why? Because if she made the squad, it would bury the voices that told me I wasn't *good enough* to cheer. I could live vicariously through her accomplishment. Ugh. I just grossed myself out.

Wanting our kids to live out our dreams, or expecting them to succeed where we've failed, puts too much pressure on them. Our intensity manifests as nagging and criticism. We micromanage so our kids make honor roll, become class president, make first chair in band, break records with SAT or ACT scores, and graduate *summa cum laude*. We want them to win, not just give a good effort. In our minds, their success reflects our good parenting.

This tangle is especially dangerous for our kids because they learn approval is based on performance. Parenting should be about encouraging their talents, building their character, and pointing them to Jesus . . . not making up for our shortcomings.

As Adults

Finding significance and value from our kids doesn't necessarily stop once they graduate from high school. It just looks different. There's still competition between parents to see whose children have successfully stepped into adulthood and whose failed to launch. We pat ourselves on the back when our kids choose "acceptable" careers and become doctors, CPAs, ministry leaders, or profitable business owners. And we question the parenting skills of those whose kids choose a different route.

We take pride in the number of grandkids we have, assuming our children's desire to be fruitful and multiply is because we set such a wonderful example. We brag about their financial successes, the size of their home, and their vacation plans, because it all points back to a job well done—at least in our opinion. Being pleased with your children is a good thing, but letting their successes or failures affect your parenting résumé isn't.

Many of us use parenting to validate our self-worth. It's a chance to feel successful. But often the motives for wanting our children to excel aren't pure. And we expect our kids to erase the messages we heard in our own childhood—the ones that said we were a disappointment. The ones that told us we weren't good enough. The messages that sank to the depths of our self-worth and left us feeling unlovable, ugly, stupid, or burdensome. But isn't that a heavy burden to place on our children?

The messages from childhood can't help but leave an impression on us. We operate out of those lies, often without even realizing it. And we forget that how we were parented back then affects how we parent our kids now—the good, the bad, and everything in between. Without our realizing it, the confidence and insecurities we brought out of childhood bleed into how we raise our own kids. Sometimes that's really wonderful, other times not so much.

Think about life in your home growing up.

Were your parents affirming?

Did your family have fun together?

Was there verbal abuse? Physical abuse? Sexual abuse?

Were your needs met?

Were you celebrated?

Did they compliment your character?

Was love based on your performance or achievements?

Did you feel supported?

Were you made to feel like an inconvenience?

Was there a lot of yelling?

Were you appreciated?

Was either parent filled with anger, bitterness, hate, or pride?

Did anyone struggle with addiction?

Did your parents encourage you to try again when you failed?

This is most certainly not an exhaustive list of questions, but it's meant to get you thinking. Were any of these painful to answer? Did good or bad memories flood back? Any revelations?

How you answered these questions is telling of how you feel about yourself. If you answered yes to "feeling appreciated," then chances are you believe you're valuable. If you answered no to being "encouraged to try again," you might not believe you have what it takes.

Look back at the list again. Do you parent your kids the same way you were parented? If you felt like an inconvenience, do your kids feel the same? If you were yelled at, are you yelling too? Are you battling the same addiction as one of your parents? Or are you overcompensating by raising your kids in the completely opposite way?

I know a woman whose dad was very verbally abusive while she was growing up. He knew her insecurities and preyed on them. Some of the words and phrases that came from his mouth—from his heart—have left deep wounds that she's still working through today. But rather than deflate her kids with her words, she has purposed to encourage them. Her kids know their value and she is intentional in using her words for good. She's doing it differently.

Another woman never felt noticed by her mom and dad. She was the youngest of four with busy parents who would leave her older sisters in charge. They missed her sporting events, her awards ceremonies, and other important parts of her life. Even now, they still forget her birthday and other notable occasions. While she knows they love her, her deepest wound is not being seen by them. But her kids are seen. She's intentional in making that a part of how she parents. And her kids know, without a doubt, they are worth noticing.

One woman's mom was terribly jealous of her success and could never bring herself to speak an honest compliment. If she chose to affirm, it was the bare minimum. This woman was thirsty to hear, "Great job," or "I'm so proud of you," but those words rarely came. So with her own kids, she looks for ways to speak approval and encouragement all the time. She doesn't get jealous of their success, she prays for it.

Many of us are still tangled up in those *not good enough* feelings from our own childhood and scared we'll send the same message to our own kids. We don't want to repeat our parents' mistakes. We don't want to be the reason our kids are on a first-name basis with their therapist. Rather than be critical, we want to guide and empower our kids to make good choices. Instead of making them feel inadequate, we want them to know they're rock stars. If they speak negatively over themselves, we want to teach them the power of words (Prov. 18:21). The good news is, we can make these changes. And it all starts with forgiveness.

Holding on to the painful messages of worthlessness from childhood is like wearing an oversized coat. It hides the real you—the you that wants to feel acceptable. Every painful comment, every hurtful look, all the times you felt like a disappointment, every time you felt insignificant, and all the other messages that made you feel unlovable are like threads woven through its fabric. Few of us are threadbare. And these heavy coats of worthlessness affect how we parent. Our words and actions reflect the cloak of wounds we wear.

Until you forgive those who spoke tangling words, you won't be free. It doesn't mean you have to reconcile, nor does it suggest that what they did was right, but it releases the knots that hold your self-esteem hostage. It gives you the confidence you need to be the mom God designed you to be.

That is, until you see *her.*

Few things can knock out the "I'm a good mom" feeling more than when I compare my worst day of parenting to someone else's best. I remember rushing around one morning, getting myself and my four- and five-year-old ready for Bible study. Because I was leading a group, I needed to be at church earlier than everyone else. And it never fails that when I'm in a hurry, everything that could happen, does.

I'd woken up late, which never starts a day off right. Plus, half of the Scott clan isn't known for cheerful morning attitudes to begin with. It was snowing, so I knew the drive would be longer and trickier. We couldn't find snow boots. I couldn't find my Bible study guide. I hated all my clothes and changed a million times. So when my youngest spilled her milk, I lost it.

I began screaming and stomping around the house. My performance was Oscar-worthy in the psycho-mom genre, and it freaked out my kids. I don't usually fly off the handle like that. At the end of my tirade, Sara was under the kitchen table crying and Sam was hiding in another room. Awesome. Not my best mommy moment. Nope, not at all.

We grabbed our coats and ran out the door. As I glanced in the backseat, I saw how miserable my kids looked. Guilt washed all over me. How could I lead a group through the Word of God after berating my kids an hour earlier?

As we were getting out of the car, I saw *her*. How did she always look so cute? Her kids were all smiles, their clothes matched, and they responded "Yes, ma'am" when she told them to behave in class. Apparently their morning had looked a bit different than ours. They hugged and kissed, and as she walked by me, she said, "Rough morning?" She wasn't trying to be demeaning; she's a sweet woman. But at that moment, I felt completely inferior.

Author and activist Dillon Burroughs says, "The problem with comparison is that you always feel either better than someone else or worthless compared to someone else."[1] Exactly. Why do we have to measure our parenting ability to another's? It's a surefire way to tangle our self-confidence.

Out of all the moms on earth, God chose you to be Mom to your kids. He knew you'd have exactly what they'd need to thrive. He uses your upbringing, life experiences, trials and tribulations, and mistakes and victories as a well of wisdom to help you parent. You're not a mom by accident.

When we trust God to untangle our parenting insecurities, it means we surrender our unrealistic expectations, our self-seeking motives, and our comparison tendencies. We work through our childhood wounds, forgiving our parents for the ways they hurt us. And when we do, everything changes because we know we don't have to be perfect parents . . . just *purposeful* ones.

Her Tangle: A Story from Katie

I've struggled with my self-worth for as long as I can remember. I feel so fortunate to have grown up in a Christian home. But it was far from perfect. My mother struggled with bipolar disorder, which went untreated for years. And both my parents had issues with codependency. Turmoil and conflict—and the feelings of insecurity and discomfort they produced—were a vivid part of my childhood.

My mother loved me, but her own limitations made her incapable of giving me the reinforcement and nurturing that I craved. I don't blame her. She was mostly just trying to survive herself. Still, it left a void—one that I quickly tried to fill by searching for validation in my performance and other people's opinions of me.

I brought that need for approval into my marriage, and then into my parenting. If I could please no one else, I was determined to please my children. If I could be the best mommy, do all the right things, and earn their undying love and gratitude, I might just be enough. I tied my value and emotional health to their view of me, their happiness, and their behavior.

Fortunately, God wouldn't have any of it. In his infinite wisdom, he gave me two incredibly strong-willed children. They didn't care much for my grand plan of "make Mommy look and feel good about herself."

These spirited kids were constantly placing me in uncomfortable situations that required me to be tough and set boundaries. I knew I should stand firm, but that meant facing conflict and risking their unhappiness with me. Those old childhood feelings of craving value and wanting to stop the turmoil—no matter what the cost—resurfaced with a vengeance. This made me angry and resentful toward my children. I constantly felt exhausted, inadequate, and like a big, fat failure.

Every time I gave in when I should have held firm left me feeling wounded and ashamed. I was determined to try harder, but my emotional energy was fading and unable to sustain me. As my children reached the adolescent years, I found that these feelings only intensified. Now they were asserting their independence and acting out in a whole new way. They frequently didn't like me. They thought I was unfair and embarrassing. Whatever was left of the shaky foundation of my self-worth just crumbled away.

In fact, those years destroyed me. In a good way. God used this incredibly difficult season in my parenting to increase my dependence on him. He opened my eyes to the foolishness of anchoring my identity to flawed humans—especially volatile teenagers. What a fool's errand that was!

I was literally brought to my knees. I guess it's human nature, but people usually don't change their behavior until they experience a fair amount of pain. I came to a place of complete exhaustion. Emotionally, I was wounded and bleeding. I was finally ready to do whatever it took to live a different way. God was so faithful to bring a friend into my life at that time who came alongside me and spoke truth to me. She held me accountable, encouraging me to make the hard, painful choices.

I finally realized—with devastating clarity—how my quest for validation was damaging my kids. They needed boundaries and stability. I had to risk being viewed as the "bad guy." Over and over again. Gradually, I found more and more strength to do it. There was no formula to how God set me free. All I know is that it started with the Holy Spirit opening my eyes. Then I just asked for his strength and leading as I took one step and then another, often with my knees knocking. Each time I set a boundary or made an unpopular decision and survived, I gained a little more strength and confidence.

During this time, I relied on Jesus and the Holy Spirit's guidance like never before. He was so sweet to me. I expected him to scold me. I waited for him to say *What took you so long?* But the condemnation never came. Step-by-step, choice-by-choice, he simply showed me a better way to live, free of fear. This newfound confidence gave me a different perspective. I was no longer driven by approval from my kids, but instead by what was truly best for them. I was able to accept God's grace and feel his very deep and real love for me as he faithfully healed my heart and answered my feeble prayers—time and time again. The more I saw his provision and experienced his very personal and practical love for me, the more I tied my value to him.

I can't tell you that all of my old patterns are gone forever—that I never fall back into old habits or unhealthy ways of thinking. I do. And, actually, I'm glad I do. It's always a potent reminder of my incredible need for a Savior who loves and values me beyond measure. And it's an opportunity to once again experience his mercy and grace.

I continue to love my children fiercely, but they're no longer the measure of my worth and effectiveness. Instead, each day, I wake up determined to tie my worth to their Creator alone. And I feel freedom.

~ Katie

His Anchor

> Don't you see that children are God's best gift?
>   the fruit of the womb his generous legacy?
> Like a warrior's fistful of arrows
>   are the children of a vigorous youth.
> Oh, how blessed are you parents,
>   with your quivers full of children! (Ps. 127:3)

Do not try to rule over those who have been put in your care, but be examples to the flock. (1 Pet. 5:3 GNT)

My child, pay attention to what your father and mother tell you. Their teaching will improve your character as a handsome turban or a necklace improves your appearance. (Prov. 1:8–9 GNT)

And show your own self in all respects to be a pattern and a model of good deeds and works, teaching what is unadulterated, showing gravity [having the strictest regard for truth and purity of motive], with dignity and seriousness. (Titus 2:7 AMP)

Train up a child in the way he should go [and in keeping with his individual gift or bent], and when he is old he will not depart from it. (Prov. 22:6 AMP)

Your Untangling Prayer

Father, help me see my kids as blessings rather than measuring sticks of my worth. So often I depend on their success or failure to gauge my significance. I know it's not healthy for either of us.

Would you untangle the guilt too? I'm always worried that I am messing up my kids. I struggle to feel like I know what I'm doing, and it shakes my self-assurance to the core. I don't want to parent out of my insecurities.

Please forgive me for trying to do this without you. Truth is, I need you to help me parent. And I know you love my kids more than I'm capable of loving them. Give me confidence to be the mom you designed me to be. Remind me that you chose me to be Mom to _____. I want to parent on purpose.

And help me know that I am valuable, and it has nothing to do with any performance or achievements from my kids. They don't complete me. You do.

Untangle me, Father.
I pray all this in the sweet name of Jesus. Amen.

Loosening the Knot Questions

1. How does your parenting style reflect the way you were raised? What do you like about it, and what part poses challenges?

2. What role does mommy-guilt play in how you parent?

3. How have you seen your child's success or failure affect your worth as a mom? What needs to change?

4. What is the Holy Spirit speaking to you right now?

Tangled in Domestic Disappointment

As Jesus and the disciples continued on their way to Jerusalem they came to a village where a woman named Martha welcomed them into her home. Her sister Mary sat on the floor, listening to Jesus as he talked. But Martha was the jittery type and was worrying over the big dinner she was preparing. She came to Jesus and said, "Sir, doesn't it seem unfair to you that my sister just sits here while I do all the work? Tell her to come and help me."

Luke 10:38–40 TLB

The *jittery type*? I love how this Bible translation describes Martha. When someone is jittery, it means they are nervous, on edge, and stressed out. Martha was a bundle of nerves about preparing this dinner for Jesus and company. And to make things worse, she was abandoned by her sister, the only help she'd have to pull this meal off without a hitch. Her insecurities were beginning to show.

I don't entertain much in my home. I'm terribly self-conscious about my cleaning and cooking abilities. I worry people will notice the dust bunnies running amok or that the meal I prepare will cause stomach issues later. What if my cats jump on the counter with company around? What if their fork has crusted green bean goop on it? Stress, stress, stress.

I'm what one would call an under-par domestic goddess. I often break into a sweat just knowing people are coming over. Being an introvert, I feel that my home is my haven—and I'd like to keep it that way. Surely I'm not the only one tangled in this struggle. Inviting people into my sacred space can be a big trigger, opening the door to all sorts of insecurities. And Martha's story proves this tangle is an age-old one.

In Luke 10 we can imagine the two sisters whistling while they worked together to clean up and make preparations for the visit. But things changed when Jesus walked in the door. Mary, the younger sister, was so overcome with his presence that she abandoned her sister and her duties. She just wanted to spend time with him. But in Martha's mind, there was too much to do and taking a break was a luxury she couldn't afford.

She needed this visit to be perfect for her guests. Martha's reputation was important, and she wanted to be known as the "hostess with the mostess." This desire tangled her up, because she believed her worth was tied to her homemaking abilities.

I imagine she worried about the food, concerned it might be overcooked or on the salty side. She might have worried the pillows weren't fluffed to plumpness. If her house wasn't clean enough or the accommodations unwelcoming, what would people say? And with Mary indisposed, Martha's reputation was on the line.

After she approached Jesus, asking him to command Mary to help her in the kitchen, he responded differently than expected. "Martha, dear Martha, you're fussing far too much and getting yourself worked up over nothing. One thing only is essential, and Mary has chosen it—it's the main course, and won't be taken from her"(vv. 41–42). Because Martha's sense of value was tied to her reputation as a hospitable hostess, she missed out on a great party.

So often, Martha gets a bad rap. How would you like your rebuke to make it into the bestselling book of all time? How about being known as the woman in Scripture who was wound up too tightly? Or what if your private conversation with Jesus was made public and regularly used in sermons as an example of what not to do?

But you know what Martha did right? She went to Jesus with her frustration. She offers us a great example of how to handle those situations where those *not good enough* feelings begin to surface. Martha was afraid the dinner might be less than perfect without her sister's help. There was a lot to do. And while she might have been in the kitchen cussing under her breath just a few minutes earlier, she didn't waste too much time before she took her anxiety straight to him.

Martha cared about the comfort of her guests. She wanted to fill their empty bellies with yummy food. Feeding these men as they were passing through her village was a ministry opportunity she took very seriously. Martha was known as being hospitable, and she tied her self-esteem to this reputation. The last thing she wanted was to disappoint her company.

I like Martha. If we're honest, we could each find a connecting point with her. Somewhere in our domestic abilities we struggle with insecurity. We worry our *not good enough* will show and embarrass us. But it helps to remember that God created us for community, not cooking. He wants us to connect, not clean. Well, while that isn't exactly sound theology, you get my point. Of course we can keep a nice house and take pride in making a good meal, but we get knotted up when those things begin to define our self-worth. And, unlike Martha, not everyone has the gift of entertaining.

Several years back, I took a spiritual gifts inventory through my church. This test helped define where my gifting might be. Based on how I answered each question, I received a numerical score for every category. I could have scored high in shepherding, visual arts, church planting, teaching, serving, or one of many other areas listed on the test.

One area was hospitality, and I scored a big fat zero. Of the several hundred questions I answered, I didn't positively respond to one question that would have scored a vote in this category. And it's not terribly surprising.

I'm always worried I will be judged for the state of my home. Will it smell like my cats? Will my guests like how I've decorated? Is the neighborhood nice enough? It's nerve-racking. While my home is usually clutter-free, it's not dust-free. And rather than take the time to wipe it away, I sometimes write words such as *joy* or *love* or *peace* in it.

Funny, I never worry about my home until someone is coming over. I love this house—everything about it. We back up to a pond in a neighborhood tucked into the foothills of Northern Colorado. The décor is exactly how we like it, and the colors reflect our personalities and taste. We have nice furniture and fun knickknacks. The size fits my family nicely, giving us plenty of room to move around without stepping on each other's toes. It's perfect. But letting others into my space is an act of vulnerability, because my home is a reflection of me. And if someone is critical of my home, it can feel so personal.

Many of you may feel completely different. You're the ones who love to entertain, and you think of everything. It's an art. You even create name cards for each place setting so guests know where they're supposed to sit. The kitchen is your favorite room in the house and you love to create new dishes. You like a clean home and a day doesn't go by that you're not tidying up after everyone. For you, there is no place like home.

Does this describe you? Well, you might be considered a domestic diva if:

You begin quoting Martha Stewart's advice to others.

You have seasonal aprons, kitchen towels, and oven mitts . . . that coordinate.

Dust is afraid of you.

You see every new recipe as a foe that must be conquered.

Your idea of date night is extreme couponing with your husband.

You have spent more than ten minutes of your life comparing one cleaning product to another.

Living in a show-ready home is more thrilling than a trip to Disneyland.

You'd choose hosting a dinner party over a spa day every time.

You consider to-do list complainers to be annoying amateurs.

You know the correct way to pronounce *fondant*.

Your collection of *Southern Living* magazines makes you a candidate for the television show *Hoarders*.

As women, we let our knack for domestic duties (or lack thereof) tangle our self-worth, and that plays out in many different ways.

Dirty Advertising

Marketers spend millions making us feel like our house isn't clean—at least not yet. Think of the television commercials and magazine ads with women pathologically obsessed with keeping their toilets sparkling clean. Really? Do we need spotless potties to make us feel good about ourselves?

Other ads show women holding two different cleaning products, debating which one will make their wood floors sparkle. Who has the time for such a dilemma anyway? And at the end of the commercial, when the kids run in and muddy those just-cleaned floors, the mom smiles and reaches for her mop. Let's be real here. If that were to happen in our home, we'd be screaming at our littles to get back outside and remove their shoes. Right?

The media portrays moms as clean freaks, making us feel guilty if we're not. While we might like our home to be fresh, we've learned to cohabitate with a certain amount of dirt. We have pets and kids and husbands, all of whom track in things we'd rather leave outdoors. Truth is, we really *live* in our home. Maybe you're different, but I don't have all day to remove every trace of it.

The Show-Me State

As I am writing this book, we're in the throes of selling our home. It's bittersweet. Like I mentioned earlier, this has been a wonderful home. But because most of our "life" is on the other side of town, we feel God calling us to move to that area. Living in a staged home, though, is a challenge. I've cleaned more in the past month than in my entire fifteen years of marriage. Okay, I just grossed myself out a bit.

This process triggers my rejection issues like nobody's business. Of course I think the house shows beautifully, but no one has made an offer yet. Am I missing something? Didn't they like my taste in paint colors? Didn't they find the carpet I spent days deciding on lush yet practical? Didn't my creative streak with the refinished kitchen cabinets wow them? Did they think I had bad taste in décor, furniture, and everything else I personally chose in my home? Ouch.

Every potential buyer who tours and decides it's not what they're looking for makes me think my sanctuary from the world isn't good enough.

Comparison Trap

Some of us might become discontent with our humble abode because we compare our home with the homes of others. It may be our friend's house, a beautifully decorated place showcased on Pinterest, or décor from a television show or movie home. Regardless, we're jealous of what they have and how they decorate.

Did you watch the hilarious sitcom in the '90s called *Friends*? Monica and Rachel had the stinkin' cutest apartment. The colors were fabulous, the furniture vintage. They had the perfect pillow and blanket combinations on the sofa and chairs. It was clean and tidy and painfully trendy. I always wanted that apartment. And while I tried to re-create it in my own place, it never looked right. My space was never as cool as theirs.

And it starts young. My daughter used to be envious of the main character's room on her favorite Disney sitcoms. These would leave her depressed because her room wasn't as fancy or as big as theirs. Think back to Hannah Montana's closet, for example. It was hidden behind a wall in her bedroom, and was ginormous. Even I wanted it.

Or maybe those hoity-toity furniture store commercials trip you up, because you know you can't afford the "good" stuff. You shop the discount home furnishing stores, and are certain everyone who walks in your home knows it.

When we envy, we rob ourselves of joy. In our minds, our stuff will never be as nice or as cool as others'. And when we try to mimic someone else's style and fail, it trips us up too. Sometimes our talent, calendar, or budget just doesn't allow it. In the end, we're left feeling inferior.

Penny-Pinching Power

Many of us find worth in how much money we're able to save the family when we shop. Few things excite me more than a 30-percent-off coupon for Kohl's, or an "exclusive for card members only" email with a secret discount not available to the masses. I love a good bargain and always look for the least expensive way to buy something. It makes me feel good about myself because I'm being wise with the family's money.

When I hit the jackpot of savings, I'll call my mom and share my coupon success. She does the same with me. But I don't share that kind of information with my husband—at least not anymore. Once I called with receipt in hand to report my ridiculous savings, and he responded with, "Well, how much did you have to spend to save that amount?" Humph. I said, "That's not the point." I was all proud and wanted a pat on the back. I wanted my thriftiness affirmed. I needed my husband to acknowledge what an awesome wife I was, but he didn't. Men. So I hung up and called my mommy for validation.

When we're frugal, bargain-hunting shoppers, it strokes our ego. But it can also knot us up in the performance tangle that says "smart women save money." When our friend finds a better deal or remembers to use her coupon by the expiration date and we don't, it can trigger guilt. We wonder how much money we could have saved had we been *smarter*. We feel guilty when we miss the lowest price of the season.

This can also give us a false sense of superiority. When we're the ones to make the great find, we often wear it like a badge of honor. When someone compliments our purse, we're quick to share the original price and how much of a discount we received. We brag about the secret online code we found that shipped our order for free. And we love how it makes us feel. It gets a little ridiculous. Since when did coupons and discount codes become measuring sticks of our domestic giftedness?

I'm All Busyness

We might even find self-worth in how much we're able to accomplish each day. These days, women are expected to have super powers. We're supposed to be able to tackle the household chores in a single bound. More than ever before, we feel pressure to pack our day with tasks. The more the merrier.

If I can rattle off a long list of accomplishments when my husband asks about my day, it feels great. I assume the list will validate my contribution to the family, and crown me Most Effective Domestic Diva. On the flip side, however, having only one or two feats to report can make me feel *lazy*.

Women are no longer only responsible for raising kids, cooking, and cleaning. These days we're expected to do it all. We pay the bills, schedule maintenance repairs, manage schedules for kids' sports and school activities, plan vacation and travel details, run errands for the family, and often work outside the home too. While our superhero cape may get tattered and dirty as we fly through our to-do list, many of us find our value in being highly efficient. And when we expect our helpfulness to quiet those *not good enough* voices, we get tangled up.

Sometimes our to-do lists produce guilt. We worry we're spending too much time managing a home and a family and should be doing spiritual housecleaning instead. I love this quote by Joyce Meyer—"Some Christians feel guilty when they are doing something that isn't 'spiritual.' Somehow or another, they feel the need to hurry through the grocery store, dash through the house cleaning, and rush through all the daily aspects of life that seem irrelevant to their faith."[1] Either way, our to-do lists can tangle us up.

Entertainer of the Year

I once knew a woman who was all about presentation. She had the finest dishes and her place settings were breathtaking. She used cloth napkins instead of paper towels. Who knew that was possible? She even had cute napkin rings that added an additional touch of class. She'd decorate her table for the season or occasion, complete with candles, bows, flowers, and the like. It was amazing.

She was the best cook ever. Some of the things she made, I'd never attempt. Most of them I couldn't even pronounce. She even grew food in her own garden and used it to make succulent dishes. I grow my veggies in the grocery store. It just seems easier that way.

Her invitations were lavish, and we often left with a parting gift. There was music, soft lighting, and a perfectly clean home. Somehow, when she gathered a group of women for dinner, her family and pets magically disappeared. Needless to say, it was always quite an event. But when she wasn't entertaining, she changed.

Her demeanor was different. The sweet "hostess with the mostess" attitude went south. Her attention to detail, the way she enjoyed taking care of others, disappeared. It was as if she found her worth in entertaining. When she was on, she shined. But when the lights were turned back up and the opportunity to impress expired, she didn't like what was left.

Sometimes we're forced into hosting. We may have the most room or be in a central location, and having family and friends over becomes more of a duty than a delight.

If we're not comfortable in the kitchen or obsessed with cleanliness, it can trigger big insecurities. We may find ourselves apologizing for the meal or making excuses for the dust. We worry the smell from a recent deposit in the litter box will wind its way into the dining room. We might point out our home's warts, certain they've already shown themselves. Our neighbor's weed-ridden yard or beat-up van embarrasses us, and we're sure everyone has noticed. Because we're the queen of the home, we feel ashamed.

Why do we let our level of domestic diva-ness determine how we feel about ourselves? In the grand scheme of things, does it really matter? Unmade bed, scuffed wood floors, dusty tables, unfluffed pillows, and dirty dishes have no say in our worth. As a matter of fact, I'm adopting a new philosophy for my own home. You can claim it as your own too. It goes something like this: I want my house to be clean enough that it's healthy, but dirty enough that we can live happy.

Your thriftiness and ability to knock out a to-do list don't make you a better person. We can't decide our value by how much we save or how much we do. Be careful not to tangle your self-worth in how you dress up your home and dinner table for a party. Philippians 2:3 says, "Don't do anything from selfish ambition or from a cheap desire to boast, but be humble toward one another, always considering others better than yourselves" (GNT). In God's economy, we find our value through humility. And we find our identity through his Son, Jesus. Alone.

Her Tangle: A Story from Jenny

To me, there's just something about making a house a home.

Whether it's picking out paint colors, looking at fabric, thumbing through the latest edition of *Better Homes and Gardens* magazine, or skimming through the thousands (upon thousands) of images on Pinterest, I take an avid interest in creating a warm environment in the place I dwell—the space my family and I call home.

Admittedly, I have a weird fascination with subway tile, grout, wall treatments, and whatever else I can use to improve my living quarters. In fact, I could spend all day walking the aisles of a home improvement store, just as a planned trip to the nearest Hobby Lobby could be deemed a major life event by yours truly.

It's just the way I'm wired.

Not all of us are like this though. Some of you might have just cringed in protest due to my revelations and the very thought of decorating one's home. Others? Maybe you're nodding in agreement right along with me.

But this little hobby of mine—this interest? Well, it's become a bit of a distraction in recent years. The creativity I wish to impose upon my home oftentimes finds me yearning for items I can't afford—drooling over furnishings that don't fit into my budget. It has me striving for a specific lifestyle and material items I wish I could own. It sees me dissecting every square foot of my humble abode and finding fault with all of it. Rather than counting the blessings to be found around every corner, I've narrowed my focus to the areas needing improvement instead.

"For where your treasure is, there your heart will be also" (Matt. 6:21 NIV).

Friends, it appears I'm placing all of my energy into something that's temporary, trivial, and veering to the extreme left of a Christ-centered life. This pastime of mine is tripping me up—it's instigating my fall. And despite my knowledge of Scripture and the teachings of Christ I cling to, I'm undeniably tangled in the fleshly desires of my heart.

Even though I know better. Even though I'm aware of what's really important.

You see, the past three years have been a series of highs and lows for my family. It's been a season filled with trials—a time of uncertainty, change, and insecurity too. It's found us moving in and out of three different homes in two different states. And due to unforeseen circumstances, this period also found us placing our newly constructed home up for sale.

Each of my children's bedrooms, the ones I had meticulously mapped out to match their personalities and interests? The ones

I stewed over and painted myself? Someone else's children would enjoy them, not mine. All of that time and effort I'd devoted into making that place a home for our family, was gone . . . just like that.

And I struggled.

Sure, I put on a good front—even managed to crack a smile or two, because I knew how blessed we were . . . and are! I mean, we had each other. And we understood that this life wasn't made for us to live comfortably, that trials were bound to happen, even when we least expected it. Just as I was fully aware that possessing a level three granite countertop wouldn't likely impress my Savior come judgment day either. But I still wanted these things. Despite all of the life lessons learned, I wanted to create the perfect environment for my kids, my husband, and myself too. I wanted my home-sweet-home.

You know, as I sit here and reflect, the wound is still fresh—the confusion still present. But God? He's got all of this. He's taking this precious family of mine (who he loves so much), and placing us where he sees fit. And me? He's working on me too. He's helped me to realize that Satan attacks in many different ways. That the Enemy is eager to take our gifts, our interests, and even our hobbies and use them against us. The Enemy's able to take what we can use for good and twist it into something dirty—tainted, even.

And we get tangled because of it.

We unintentionally make trivial things our idols—things that distract us from what's really important. Insignificant items like tile, drapes, paint colors, and fabric? No matter the objects, they can hold a firm grip on our focus. They can take our attention off of who and what is most important, and place it onto something that's not.

They can mess with us pretty badly, amen?

So, how do we fix it? How do you and I take these idols we've erected an altar to in our heads and do away with them? How do we recover once we've gotten stuck? How do we fixate more on Jesus and less on the stuff around us?

I ask these questions because we all suffer from these issues in one way or another. Sure, you could probably care less about the latest trends streaming online or printed in the designer magazines, because for you, it might be something else—something different. We can get tripped up in so many different ways, friend.

But here's what I know for sure: I am so much more than the contents of my house. I am so much more than stunning cabinets, gorgeous textiles, and a new front door too. My value . . . my approval? It doesn't lie in crown molding, a stone fireplace, or thousand-thread-count sheets. My home doesn't become beautiful by the number of things I place inside it. Rather, a house is made a home by the family members who live there, the faith that dwells within them, and the moments they spend together. It's within these walls—this shelter—I speak of where we must honor Christ, live out our faith, raise our children, and enjoy our days.

Sister, our homes become sweet by the love we fill them with—the love that is shared there—and the people with whom we share it.

"Let the message of Christ dwell among you richly as you teach and admonish one another with all wisdom through psalms, hymns, and songs from the Spirit, singing to God with gratitude in your hearts" (Col. 3:16 NIV).

༄ Jenny

༄ His Anchor ༄

God's people will be free from worries, and their homes peaceful and safe. (Isa. 32:18 GNT)

Be ready with a meal or a bed when it's needed. Why, some have extended hospitality to angels without ever knowing it! (Heb. 13:2)

Open your homes to each other without complaining. Each one, as a good manager of God's different gifts, must use for the good of others the special gift he has received from God. (1 Pet. 4:9–10 GNT)

After all, every house has a builder, but the builder of everything is God. (Heb. 3:4 GW)

──────ℓℓ Your Untangling Prayer ℘──────

Dear Lord,

My self-worth has been tangled in domestic disappoint-ment. I try to feel better about myself through my ability to run the home, and I'm weary. I understand how much this has played a part in my striving to feel valuable, but it's kept me on the treadmill of performance and I want to get off.

I don't want to be measured by my cooking and cleaning, my efficiency and thriftiness, or my entertaining abilities. I want to be free from the expectations that come with those things.

Forgive me for looking other places for my self-worth. I'm sorry that I've let the world define me through my domestic capabilities. Would you please remove the knots that have kept me in bondage? I want to enjoy creating and running a home for the right reasons rather than live in fear of how it will make me look.

Untangle me, Father.

I pray all this in the sweet name of Jesus. Amen.

──────ℓℓ Loosening the Knot Questions ℘──────

1. What do you enjoy the most about running a home? What do you enjoy least?

2. What responsibilities in the home make you feel the best about yourself? Why?

3. What responsibilities cause stress and worry? Why?

4. What is the Holy Spirit speaking to you right now?

Friendship: Tried, True, or *Tangled*?

"Mom, I hate her and I wish she'd just move back to where she came from. She's making my life miserable at school!" My daughter wasn't a happy camper. "She's doing all she can to split up me and my friends, and I just want to smack her!" Yep, she's mine. My daughter has that same fiery passion I do. And her situation at school not only wrecked her but me too.

I know my daughter isn't perfect. I know the catty and stinky things she's capable of doing to others. She came from me. Enough said? But I also know when my daughter isn't being a drama-llama, as we call it. Because I was having to coach my daughter through this crunchy situation almost daily, suggesting all sorts of ways to navigate it, I knew things were pretty rough.

Honestly, I'm okay with my kids struggling with friendships. It's normal and healthy, and I appreciate the opportunity to equip them now for relationships throughout their lives. While boys can fight one day and be fine the next, girls are a different breed. We can be so driven by emotion that logic never enters the picture.

I know this young girl, and I know her family too. They've been in a rough season for years now, and it's taking a toll on the whole crew. While I've not walked a mile in their shoes, I know the journey has been rocky and muddy and uphill. This family has been through more than most, and I have great compassion for them. But when she upped the game by tearing down my daughter, tangling her self-esteem with words and actions, I upped it too.

God recently revealed that my mamma-bear reaction to girl-drama comes from my own brokenness. *Ugh, why does it always seem to point back to me?* My roar is fueled by a collection of wounds inflicted by other women. So when my daughter feels the pain of rejection or worthlessness, my insecurities get triggered. Those familiar feelings flood back. And as I wipe away my daughter's tears and listen as she cries it out, I realize how easily I can relate to her.

I'm a visual learner. So when a friend offered me a visual of why I get triggered by my daughter's friendship struggles, it made complete sense. She said that when our feelings get hurt, it's like an arrow that's been shot straight into our heart. These arrows are lies from the Enemy aimed at our self-worth. Maybe the arrow says you're not good enough. Maybe it's that you're unlovable. Maybe it's that you're not worth their time. Or it could be a million other *not good enough* messages. The problem is, these arrows anchor in our self-confidence.

Rather than ask Jesus to remove them, we let them stick out from our chests. And when others bump into those arrows, the pain is fresh again. Every time someone stirs up feelings of inadequacy, the arrow of *not good enough* gets thumped. When we feel left out, the arrow of *unlovable* reverberates. When someone doesn't respond to your hurt, the arrow of *not worth their time* gets whacked. The vibrations of those thumps sink deep into our heart, making it turn black and blue.

So often the arrow that hit my daughter's heart thumps my own. I sure didn't see this coming. She'll start unpacking how mean so-and-so was on the playground, or how so-and-so started spreading lies about her, or how that group completely ignored her, and the arrows still lodged in my own heart get walloped without warning. Her pain will trigger my own.

I'll remember times I've felt like I was too much or too little. It will remind me of unmet expectations or unkind words. Memories of broken trust and burning jealousy will come back. I'll think back to seasons where I was parched for friendship, rejected by those I thought were my friends. Chances are your arrows have been thumped by another's journey too.

The truth is, we're tricky birds. Few things can mangle our confidence like hurt received from another woman. Their words—or lack thereof—can make us feel horribly inadequate. One sideways look can make us feel stupid, or a flip of hair can trigger feelings of inferiority. Alliances can change without warning, making us feel vulnerable about the secret things we shared. When the invite doesn't come, we feel left out. When the call isn't returned, we feel rejected.

But on the other hand, other women can also breathe life into our weary bones. They're the ones who steady us when life gets shaky, and remind us of who we are and whose we are when we forget. Girlfriends can dissect issues like no one else, ruminating over them for hours. They understand the complexities of hormones, and can safely ask if those might be the cause of our wonky mood—something no man can do and live.

I'm in a season of deep friendships right now, and it's beautiful. I hope you are too. If so, don't take it for granted. Relish this time because it's not always so sweet. Few things can knot us up like friendships. And the tangle tightens where the strands of delight and distress meet.

Let me give you an example of this tension. Bear with me. I am a big fan of dried apple chips. I love them. Most of the time I try to avoid foods with added sugar, so this is the perfect snack. They are sweet and crunchy and make me a happy camper. And you know that old adage, "An apple a day keeps the doctor away." This yummy fruit rocks my world. It delights me.

One day, I was watching a movie and munching away. Before I realized it, I'd eaten almost the whole bag. The packaging boasts, "Each bag has 72 apples!" I knew I was going to be in trouble.

My stomach began to bloat and I soon had horrible gas pain. My delight soon turned to distress. TMI? How could something so awesome cause me such discomfort? And when the pain intensified, my husband asked, "Are the apples worth it?" In the same way, we often question our need for community—the community that's wonderful one day but can cause grief and sorrow the next.

My mantra used to be, "I love God, just not his people." Based on my past wounds, I felt justified in closing my heart to others. It was just safer that way. But behind those words was fear that I wasn't worth loving. It was easier on my already fragile self-esteem to close the door before it could slam in my face again. I couldn't risk opening myself up to deep, intimate friendships because I'd been hurt so much in the past. And while my heart ached for community, I was also deathly afraid of it.

Friendship was thought up by God, the giver of all *delightful* things. His plan is for us to live in a cooperative spirit. He commands us to love and serve one another. God expects us to journey through life together because his heart is for community. In his book *Life Together*, Dietrich Bonhoeffer agreed.

> It is easily forgotten that the fellowship of Christian brethren is a gift of grace, a gift of the Kingdom of God that any day may be taken from us, that the time that still separates us from utter loneliness may be brief indeed. Therefore, let him who until now has had the privilege of living a common Christian life with other Christians praise God's grace from the bottom of his heart. Let

him thank God on his knees and declare: It is grace, nothing but grace, that we are allowed to live in community with Christian brethren.[1]

This quote is a great reminder that friends are God's gift to us. They make us laugh when we're down, counsel us when we're confused, direct us when we're lost, help us when we're overwhelmed, and pray for us when we're hurting. We can safely ask "Does this make my butt look big" and know they will be honest.

Friends will love us through bad haircuts and understand the tears when we get them. They'll listen for as long as we need to talk, and comfort us with, "Oh, honey." When we feel defective they'll cup our face in their sweet hands and remind us how wonderful we are. And they're the ones who know exactly what's on our mind with one glance from across the room. Oh, girlfriends are priceless. And it's so important that we understand that. Many women go through life without any deep friendships. They aren't perfect, but they are a gift.

What women do you consider precious in your life? What is it about them that rocks your world? This week, let those friends know just how special they are. Remember, you're a gift to them too.

～ ～ ～

God, in his immeasurable kindness, blesses us with women to help us journey through life. I have had some amazing friends in my lifetime, divinely inspired relationships at just the right time and in the right season.

I can think of one friend who stayed after others had gone home and held my hand as I got an IV in preparation for a CAT scan. Needles unnerve me. Another friend gave up her Sunday to counsel me off the ledge when I was hurt and angry. My old small group threw me a birthday party complete with my favorite food and presents even though I had stepped out several months earlier. A friend from college came out of nowhere and paid my fee for a training conference—and it was not cheap. Yes, God has used women to speak value and worth into my life countless times. Chances are you have women who do the same for you too. *Thank you, Lord, for these gifts.*

But do you ever wonder why God doesn't make the gift of community easier? Sure, it can be manageable when we keep friends at a surface level. We can talk recipes and favorite movies and weather all day without arguing or picking up an offense. No one will get bent out of shape if my favorite meatloaf recipe calls for more ketchup than theirs. If I'm Team Edward and my friend is Team Jacob, it won't be a deal-breaker. I might like the cooler weather and she is a sun-worshiper, but we won't mud wrestle over whose weather pattern is the best.

When we don't invest time and emotions, there's little cost and little lost. For so many of us, this describes our strategy plan to a tee. When we risk nothing and play it safe with our hearts, we rarely get hurt. But we don't get the really good stuff either.

It's when we find those deep-water friends—the ones who want to know your heart—that we feel seen and appreciated. They care about your day-to-day life. These are the friends who extend grace after your snarky comment and are quick to forgive when you lash out in anger. Like anything precious, they're a rare find. And when they come into your life you can't help but feel blessed. Can I brag? God has given me some amazing friends in the past several years. While some are in the same life stage as me—midforties, married with kids, same community—many are not. Some are older or younger than me. Some haven't yet married. Some are childless. Some are in different churches and denominations. Some live in different cities and states. Some I see only once or twice a year. But they all have two things in common: they love the Lord and they remind me I'm good enough. With these friends, the investment is big and the payoff is bigger. But so is the risk of getting hurt.

Friendship seemed less of a tangled mess when I was younger. Was it the same for you? When we hurt each other's feelings we'd apologize quickly, and we'd rarely hold grudges for more than twenty-four hours. So often, all we needed to patch up our hearts was a bowl of ice cream, a good night's sleep, or a new lip gloss. Bonnie Bell Lip Smacker, bubble gum flavor, usually did the trick.

As we got older though, the way we related to each other changed because boys entered the picture. My mom used to say, "Boys will come and go, but friends last forever." Only the first part of that proved to be true. I cringe thinking of all the friends I betrayed during those years. It seemed no friendship was sacred when cute boys were involved. We all bought a one-way ticket to Hormone-ville, population: everyone in puberty.

It was in those years we decided that girls couldn't be trusted. We made an agreement with ourselves that to protect our self-esteem we had to look out for number one. We learned the hard way to guard our own hearts, because nobody else would. Sure, we formed alliances, but those didn't stop the gossip, backstabbing, or other forms of betrayal. Our groups had revolving doors, and rather than stick together as a gender we became catty with one another. We'd take pleasure in watching him dump her because in our opinion, she deserved it. We thought nothing of spreading rumors, embarrassing the competition, breaking promises, and manipulating others, all so we'd feel better about ourselves. How did any of us come out alive?

We labeled people too. There was the smelly kid, the fat kid, the nerd, and the dork—titles few self-esteems could survive. Not all were bad. If you were a jock or a snob, you were part of the popular, cool crowd. But even those labels carried their own set of unrealistic expectations and a performance-based sense of worth. There were a myriad of other labels that stuck to us through our school years. Some even followed us into our adult lives.

Sometimes I wonder how much healthier our self-worth would be today if we'd been more careful with each other's hearts during those formative years. We didn't applaud individuality. Instead, we pointed out characteristics and features that made others different. And many of us adopted those *not good enough* messages, deciding we'd always be inadequate.

My son came home frustrated from school because a group of boys were picking on him. When I asked if he was okay, he said, "Yep. Those boys are going to end up working for me one day—if they're lucky." I might have come out of my school years stronger if I'd had that kind of confidence in myself. I walked into middle school feeling worthless and limped out of high school certain of it.

And you know what? Little has changed. Even today, our sense of value gets knotted up by our friendships.

Unrealistic Expectations

Oh girls, aren't we all guilty of expecting our friends to be what we need, when we need it? If we're not careful, our expectations will translate as demands for our friends to be available.

We'll measure their loyalty by how much time they give us and will be offended when it's less than we want. We will count on them to be where we need them, when we need them. And when they fail us, it'll push our rejection button. We might feel abandoned or not worth their time. Maybe we've tried to be manipulative by making them feel bad for not being there for us, but it backfired when they saw right through it. We can come off as too needy.

So often we fail to realize we all have our own set of responsibilities such as families, jobs, and chores. When friends expect friends to usurp the natural order of things, it's unrealistic and feelings get hurt.

Other times the problem with unrealistic expectations is that we expect deep friendship too quickly. We live in an *I-want-it-now* world that tells us waiting for anything is wrong. It's taught us to expect instant everything. Just the other day, I told my husband that our next house needs to have a double microwave instead of a double oven. And I meant it. We don't like to wait for anything.

Have you been frustrated by a five-minute wait for your cup of coffee? Do you usually pay the extra fee for overnight delivery? What about your favorite book? Did you drive to the store to buy it or download it immediately on your e-reader? It's kind of crazy when you think about it, right?

Well, we expect our friendships to be the same way. We want immediate intimacy and loyalty, and don't understand that relationships take time to build. Aristotle nailed it when he said, "Wishing to be friends is quick work, but friendship is a slow ripening fruit."[2] It's true. But we think that because we're the same gender, our relationships with each other should be easy and automatic. So we sit across the table from our new friend and purge the painful details of our lives. But their wide eyes, gaping mouth, and unreturned phone calls leave us feeling rejected.

Ugh. Been there, done that, got the T-shirt. It's important to remember that deep friendships are not a "just add water" recipe. Building trust takes consistent behavior over time. And it's unrealistic to expect any relationship to be different.

Maybe you're on board with the take-it-slowly approach because you've been wounded by a friend and are now overly cautious. Your expectation is to never be hurt again. While that's a wonderful hope and desire, it's not realistic.

I've most certainly hurt my friends before. A careless statement, forgetting to return a call, misinterpreted body language, a lack of discernment, an angry response. You name it, I've done it.

Offending others is, unfortunately, just part of the human condition. So is the capacity to forgive. As long as you know your friend's heart for you is good, that her wounding wasn't malicious, release her from having to be perfect. It will deepen the friendship and strengthen your confidence.

This has been a tough knot for God to untangle in my life. I've learned that many of the demands I placed on my friends have been unfair and unrealistic. My feelings would get hurt when no one would come watch me speak at an event. I thought that since they were my friends, they'd want to support me. I mean, isn't that what friends do?

But I realize now that my worth was tangled in my expectation of their presence. My thought was, *If they valued our friendship and cared for me, they'd be here.* And when they weren't, my feelings were hurt and another brick was placed on the wall that protected my heart.

What knotted me up was that I didn't recognize all the ways my friends did support me. They prayed for me, texted me encouragement, and followed up after the event to get the skinny. Expecting them to follow me from venue to venue was selfish and unrealistic. These women had their own families and careers to corral.

We also sometimes forget that relationships have a natural ebb and flow to them. There are seasons where I talk to my besties a lot and other times where we go weeks without a meaningful connection. That's normal. With all the responsibilities that fill our days, we just don't have time for epic phone conversations or three-hour coffee dates on a regular basis.

But it's so easy to be offended. It's easy to feel slighted when friends don't do what we expect of them. Part of the untangling process is letting God untie those expectations from our friends and anchor them to him instead. While your needs may be unrealistic to others, they aren't to God. Let that sink in a moment.

You will never be too needy for God. He won't ever grow weary of your insecurities. When you realize you're expecting too much from friends, say this out loud: *My expectations aren't unrealistic to God. He wants to meet each one of them.* And you know what? He is the only one who can.

Jealousy

Insecurity is at the center of the jealousy knot. It's the feeling that reminds us we're not good enough. It drives us to discontentment because we want what she has—be it her figure, her marriage, her home, her résumé, or the like. And if we could just get *it*, life would be better.

Think about it though. Are you willing to do what she had to do to get it? Will you put in the time, the cash, the training, or the effort? I have a sweet friend who has an amazing body. She is fit, strong, and tan, and nothing jiggles when she walks. Well, maybe her cute hair, but nothing else. If I'm not careful, I will get tangled up in jealousy over how she looks. But then I realize I don't want to work out like she does. Plus, I like my chips and salsa and my sweet tea. And my secret stash of chocolate.

When we become envious of our friends, we create an emotional distance between us. We see them as *better than* and ourselves as *less than*, giving them a position of power in our friendship—power they may not even realize they have. It takes the relationship from an alliance and twists it into a competition, even if only in our own minds. And in every competition there is a winner and a loser.

I've watched this happen in my own life and it destroyed a friendship very dear to my heart. Rather than cheer me on, my friend became envious of how God was moving in my life. He was opening doors for my ministry that she felt should have been opened for her instead. She was my closest friend at the time, and I couldn't share this promotion with her. Our friendship became awkward and distant. And we were never able to recover from it.

Jealousy happens when we look outward, but it's actually an inward response to our own insecurity. This selfish emotion can destroy a friendship or cause deep discontentment. It might look like this . . .

As you head out the door to meet your friend for coffee, you're anxious about the big zit on your chin, certain everyone will notice it. She sits across from you with her nauseatingly flawless complexion and all you can think about is how to get her skin. Rather than be happy acne isn't a struggle for her, you become frustrated because it is for you.

Or you notice how attentive your friend's husband is. He hugs her, brings flowers home, and calls throughout the day, and you wish your husband was more that way. Rather than recount all the amazing things about your man, you start a list of his shortcomings. By the end of the day, you're angry at him and jealous of her.

Maybe you're envious of your friend's social calendar. She is constantly meeting others for lunch or a girls' night out, and you spend your evenings watching *Jeopardy* reruns with a cat in your lap. Every time she shares about her outings, you feel more and more jealous and less and less valued. It makes you wonder, *What's wrong with me? Why don't I get invited out too?*

Someone once told me that comparison is the death of joy. Ain't that the truth? I'm the most unhappy with who I am when I start comparing myself to my friends, because the measuring criteria I use isn't fair. God made us different on purpose, so I can't accurately compare apples to oranges—me to her. And when I do it anyway, I rarely come out on top.

God has been untangling this for me. I've found peace in understanding that someone will always be skinnier, smarter, funnier, and better dressed, with better hair, than me. Others will have more money, take fancier vacations, drive more expensive cars, and have a bigger home. Certain friends will cook better, entertain with more flair, volunteer more often, have a sweeter disposition, and offer wiser advice. Those differences should be celebrated rather than compared. Until we choose to see their *better thans* as blessings instead of measuring sticks, jealousy will tangle our friendships.

Confidence Killers

Some of our deepest wounds have come from other women. We've all felt the pain of a friendship gone bad at some point in our lives. As a matter of fact, I bet while reading this chapter you've already thought of at least one situation where your trust was shattered by a friend. While we may be able to forgive, chances are we rarely forget. But that doesn't stop us from longing for the thing that has hurt us the most.

When God created us, he installed a desire for companionship. He knew we'd need others. You see his understanding in Genesis 2: "Now the Lord God said, It is not good (sufficient, satisfactory) that the man should be alone; I will make him a helper (suitable, adapted, complementary) for him" (v. 18 AMP).

This verse may be in context of husband and wife, but it proves that God knew we'd long for camaraderie. It's natural for us to want friends even if we've been deeply hurt by someone in the past. We get into trouble, though, when we don't choose wisely because our self-esteem is at risk. God asks us to love and forgive, but we can do so with healthy boundaries in place.

There are four types of friends that are confidence killers.

Negative Nellies
Backstabbers
Look-at-Mes
Unavailables

Because these kinds of friends are careless with our feelings, they have the power to make us feel worthless. My advice? Run away—and fast. I'm not trying to sound callous or graceless, but it's important we form healthy friendships with women who will care for our hearts. Not perfectly, of course, but purposefully.

Without a doubt, we've all had these kinds of friends at one time or another. Maybe you'll recognize your current friends in this list, knowing changes need to take place. Maybe God will reveal why past friendships hurt so much. Or maybe God will show you where you're hurting your friends. Let's take a look.

Negative Nellies

These women are quick to point out where you're wrong. They rarely like your choice of clothes or how you've colored your hair. They notice your dirty home and can always suggest a better way to make the soup. Rather than acknowledge your victories, they comment on your shortcomings—all in love, of course.

These friends are ready to offer advice on how things should have been handled differently—better. They're critical, judgmental, and speak truth without love. And so often they believe they're doing us a favor by sharing their thoughts and suggestions.

You might hear comments like, "It could have been tastier if . . ." or "I would have handled it differently," or even "Maybe try it this way next time." Instead of compliment, they critique. Rather than encourage, they evaluate. Where they could praise, they point the finger instead. In their opinion, the cup is always half empty and the world is going to perdition in a handbag.

To add insult to injury, these friends withhold kind words. They think they're saving us from self-absorption by offering only a morsel of praise for a job well done. They willingly pass on the opportunity to encourage a friend who needs to know what they've done is good enough.

As women, we want to be seen. We want others to notice when we meet a goal and celebrate when we overcome an obstacle. We need friends who affirm us as we journey through life. It's a privilege to breathe life into a friend who needs to know she matters. But negative Nellies won't be the ones to do it.

Backstabbers

Betrayal cuts to the core because you don't see it coming. One moment you're sharing your private struggle with a friend, and the next it becomes public knowledge. So often, it's shared under the guise of a prayer request. "Did you hear that Becky's husband is having an affair? Let's tell the small group so we can all be praying for her."

Author Toba Beta once said, "Friendship's enemy is betrayal."[3] It's true, because friendship is rooted in trust. And once broken, you are left questioning your value to that friend.

I remember a time someone was disloyal to me. She had been a sounding board during a frustrating season in my life. We talked about my struggle openly. In hindsight, I should have been more discerning in our conversations, but I wasn't. And just a few weeks later, someone else confronted me about what I had shared in confidence.

While the betrayal hurt, there was genuine repentance. She was heartsick about letting me down, and working through that one incident has made our friendship even stronger. I know how much I matter to her, and today I trust her with my heart.

Not only have I been the victim of a backstabber but I've been the one left holding the knife. Sometimes the news just compels you to share it. Chances are you've been on both sides of this one too. We're human, we will mess up, and trust can be restored. But chronic backstabbers are a different breed because it's their normal modus operandi, and it usually doesn't take their friends long to discover it.

At the core, gossiping about someone's struggles gives them a feeling of superiority. They're privy to information others aren't, or are the first to know when a life storm rocks someone's boat. But what they don't understand is the devastating message their gossip sends to the betrayed. It says, *Now that your insecurities or failures or fears have been exposed, others won't like what they see.*

These types of women may honestly want your friendship, but there's a disconnect in how to walk it out. And when you confront them, they either deny any wrongdoing or apologize profusely, promising to never hurt you again. But they will.

Look-at-Mes

These are the friends who live in the it's-all-about-me-niverse and don't even know it. They hog the spotlight, monopolize the conversation, and rarely stop talking long enough to ask anything about your life. You may know A through Z about this woman, but she doesn't even know your favorite coffee drink or the ages of your kids.

Look-at-Mes are self-centered, narcissistic, and egocentric. Social media is their favorite megaphone to brag about their great lives, amazing marriages, and perfect kids. In person, their endless self-promotion can suck the life out of your sense of worth because your life, your story, and your challenges don't get any air time.

Without speaking the words themselves, their message is *You don't matter, but I most certainly do.*

Unavailables

When you need a sounding board, these friends aren't around. You text, you call, you email, but their response remains the same—*Sorry, I can't chat right now. But I'll be praying!* They claim to be close friends, but when the going gets tough, the unavailables stay away.

This kind of friendship sends the message that you're not worth their effort. Their lack of engagement says they don't have time for you, and won't make it either. Your relationship is good as long as your life is good. But when life gets messy, rest assured the unavailables won't be in the mix.

While friendship can trigger all sorts of insecurities, God created it to be a gift. We get into trouble when we turn it from a gift into a gauge of our worth. If you ask him to untangle your self-esteem from those unhealthy places in your friendship, he will. God is the only One who can work out those knots.

Her Tangle: A Story from Jill

When I was younger, my friends would often compliment me on how quiet I was, what a good listener I was, how understanding and empathetic I was, and how easy I was to get along with. I always took those words to heart and wanted to be the kind of person anyone could come and talk to.

What I didn't realize was that over time, this started to define in my own mind who I was and where my worth came from. Somewhere along the line I began believing that if I wasn't the quiet person everyone thought I was, I'd be rejected and people would no longer want to spend time with me. In my mind, my self-worth came from being the shoulder people could cry on. Outside of that, I didn't see much more I could offer my friends.

Like all of my other friends, I had struggles too. I was just as messy on the inside as they were. And while I assumed others could see it, I didn't think it mattered to them. My role was the quiet girl who was there for everyone else. I was affirmed for that. So I slowly began letting go of any expectation that my friends would care what was going on in me. I was accepted because of my meekness, and I wasn't about to rock the boat.

As time went on, I became even quieter, especially around people with strong personalities. I didn't feel I was good enough to join in the conversation. What would people think if I shared my opinion? With my self-esteem tangled in being seen and not heard, I was fearful of ever opening my mouth to disagree with anyone.

I'm not sure how it started, but I found myself so knotted up in the pursuit of acceptance and approval of others that I wasn't sure who I was anymore. I felt like a fraud. I had all sorts of ideas and opinions on the inside but rarely voiced them. On the outside I appeared agreeable, a trait I knew would ensure that others liked me.

Fast-forward a couple years to a time right after graduating from college and having just met my soon-to-be husband. Being loved and wanted by someone who I felt saw the real me was the springboard I needed to start my untangling journey. God used this wonderful man to show me I could be loved and accepted for who I was. I didn't have to hide in my shell. I didn't have to stay silent. I didn't have to bury my needs. My voice mattered!

As the years have gone by, I've grown and matured. A lot. And I genuinely like who I am. I can hardly believe that I allowed the acceptance of my friends to so completely define who I was. While I know that was never their intention—they are amazing people—I wish I would have been more confident and able to show them all of me. But because they affirmed that one part of me, I decided that was what made me valuable.

Being trapped in fear was exhausting. Trying to play the perfect friend, the perfect person, made me resentful. I was afraid of being rejected so I chose to not be vulnerable. I was striving for love and acceptance, and placed unrealistic expectations on myself. And for most of my school career, I struggled to see myself as worthy at all.

God is still growing me in this area. I'm learning that I need to be vulnerable with others, to show who I am and risk rejection even if I'm afraid. In her book *Daring Greatly*, author Brene Brown shares how years of research have shown her that being vulnerable is essential to living a wholehearted life. She also recognizes that vulnerability with others is one of the most prevalent fears across the board. Is it something you struggle with? Well, friend, you're not alone.

We all worry about the consequences of opening ourselves up to others, whether it's our spouse or our friends. Don't we want to be liked, loved, and accepted? But in order to truly be any of those things, we must first be ourselves. We must find our worth through God's eyes. We must ask him to untangle those insecurities that keep us knotted up in fear. Only then can we truly find life.

~ Jill

His Anchor

> You use steel to sharpen steel,
> and one friend sharpens another. (Prov. 27:17)

And let us consider each other carefully for the purpose of sparking love and good deeds. Don't stop meeting together with other believers, which some people have gotten into the habit of doing. Instead, encourage each other, especially as you see the day drawing near. (Heb. 10:24–25 CEB)

Friends always show their love. (Prov. 17:17 GNT)

Laugh with your happy friends when they're happy; share tears when they're down. Get along with each other; don't be stuck-up. Make friends with nobodies; don't be the great somebody. (Rom. 12:15–16)

Friends mean well, even when they hurt you. But when an enemy puts his arm around your shoulder—watch out! (Prov. 27:6 GNT)

Your Untangling Prayer

Father, thank you for the gift of community. While it doesn't always feel like a blessing, your Word confirms it is. Would you please help me understand your plan for it in my life, so I can be confident in it?

I know community is important, but sometimes it's so hard to navigate my friendships well. I've been hurt and need you to make me wholehearted again. Please help me.

I confess I'm jealous of _____ because she _____. Give me the eyes to see your blessings in my life. Thank you for making me on purpose. Help me love who I am and what I have, and remove any discontentment from my heart. Lord, thank you for my friend, and I ask you to richly bless her life.

I confess that I have unrealistic expectations of _____ by wanting her to _____. Help me forgive her for not meeting my needs, something she was never meant to do. Please remind me to trust you instead. Lord, I release her from being my savior.

And Father, I've been so wounded by women in the past. That pain has kept me from experiencing healthy friendships now. Help me forgive _____ for _____ so I can walk in freedom. I bless her and release her.

But most of all, keep me from finding my sense of value in my friendships. Lord, I'm asking you to untie my self-esteem from community and anchor it in Jesus. Remind me who I am and whose I am so I don't look for significance in unhealthy places. Untangle me, Father.

I pray all this in the sweet name of Jesus. Amen.

ꠥ Loosening the Knot Questions ꠥ

1. How have the unrealistic expectations you've placed on your friends affected your self-esteem? How does God want you to change this?

2. How has jealousy in friendships made you feel not good enough?

3. What wounds from friends are you still holding on to? How do they affect your confidence and self-worth in your friendships today?

4. What is the Holy Spirit speaking to you right now?

The *Tangled* Web
of Social Media

Every morning was the same routine. My alarm would scream and I'd roll over, grab my phone, and lie in bed checking all of the numbers associated with my social media accounts—the ones that affirmed or deflated my self-esteem. My insecurity gave those numbers the power to decide if I would walk into my day confident or limp into it defeated.

If anyone on Facebook had de-friended me overnight, I began to panic, wondering what I had done to offend them. I'd feel guilty for posting something that upset them, and trying to figure out what it was unraveled me. Since I didn't get notifications, I would have no idea which friend had broken up with me. I just knew I had fewer friends than I did the day before. Ugh. It was a huge trigger for my tangle of shame and guilt. As much as I tried to find acceptable excuses—a glitch in the system, a closed account, an accidental rejection—I ruminated over what the "real" reason could be.

The amount and type of interaction on my wall caused issues too. I'd check my most recent status update to see how many people *liked* what I had to say. And when they shared it with their people, it satisfied something in me. I felt smart and clever, and it was a huge boost for my self-esteem. I was share-worthy, and it felt good!

From there, I'd jump to my ministry page on Facebook. I was trying to grow my platform—a fancy word for the number of people who find you worthy of following—and this number was especially important to me. I used it to validate the calling God had placed on my life. If someone cared enough to click the *Like* button, I must be doing something right. But if I lost a fan, it messed with my mind. And believe me, my mind is a scary place to begin with. I was knotted up before I was even properly caffeinated.

Next was Twitter. I'd check retweets and confirm if my following was holding steady or not. I then clicked to LinkedIn to monitor my number of connections, and then moved on to Pinterest. Of all the social media out there, this was my favorite. I'd usually spend a little extra time here keeping an eye on my repins, comments, and likes for each pin . . . and checking out the latest peanut butter dessert recipes. Seriously yum, but I digress.

The madness would come to a close with a quick look at my blog and all the stats that surrounded it—number of page views, what content had the most hits, how many comments my latest post received, and so on. It all mattered. It all counted. And the question that started each day was, *Will I get out of bed feeling good about myself—relevant, lovable, and worthy—or will I walk into the world feeling, once again, not good enough?*

It might seem silly that those online numbers had such power over how I felt about myself, but I have a hunch I'm not alone. Using Facebook, Twitter, LinkedIn, Pinterest, personal blog stats, or other social media as a measuring stick for our self-worth is becoming an epidemic among men and women alike. Chances are you know exactly what I mean because it's woven a web of worthlessness in you too. What social media numbers give you the most grief? Maybe the question should be which ones *don't*.

Maybe it's not the numbers that trip you up; it's the nauseatingly perfect lives of others. Their updates and photos make you feel *less than* them. And to add salt to the wound, you get to read about their success every time you log on. It reinforces those *not good enough* feelings with reminders that you can't compete with them.

When was the last time you read someone's status update about their kids and it made you want to puke? Maybe their daughter received higher grades than yours, or their son plays a sport you wished your son was interested in. They go on and on about their amazing children, giving a laundry list of achievements.

In photos, these prodigies are perfectly dressed in the latest fashion and their smiles tell the tale of the happiest children alive. Inside, you feel inferior because your child is just *average*. Your offspring lack the extraordinary superpowers of *her* children. And you ask yourself, *What am I doing wrong?*

Maybe you're nauseated by reading romantic engagement updates or sappy anniversary posts. It's just another fabulous reminder that you're alone. If you see another "Ten years ago I married my best friend" or "I am the luckiest woman alive!" or "It was the most perfect proposal ever" update, you might take out a whole gallon of ice cream yourself.

As much as you'd like to celebrate with them, they have what you desperately want. And their photos and comments unknowingly rub your nose in it. You're left wondering if it will ever be your turn. You ask, *Why not me? Am I not worthy to be loved?*

Maybe you're struggling to lose weight or stick to an exercise plan, and reading tweets and posts about how easy it is for others whispers *failure* into your self-confidence. When your friend posts her before-and-after photos bragging about her success, it's a painful reminder of your disappointment. You think, *Why don't I have her results? Why does it come so easy for her but not for me?*

Rather than count your blessings, you count calories. Instead of reaching out to friends, you reach for your running shoes. And when your resolve doesn't pay off, you choke on an oversized helping of underachiever's guilt. *Why is my best not good enough?*

Or maybe you found a recipe on Pinterest that boasts *easy*, step-by-step instructions for the birthday cake to end all birthday cakes; one that promises to make you mom of the year. And although you followed the recipe to a tee, your creation looks more like an Impressionist painting by Monet than something from Rachel Ray's kitchen. In the end, it reinforces that your best efforts aren't good enough, and you feel like a culinary catastrophe. *I can't even follow a recipe.*

A friend and I were just talking about the Pinterest phenomenon and how it negatively impacts how we feel about ourselves. It might be the biggest guilt-producing social media out there. How many crafts or recipes have you attempted that looked or tasted *nothing* like promised? Yeah, me too.

We've all seen it. Rather than run to the local bakery to buy birthday cupcakes for their children, women are walking into school classrooms with over-the-top masterpieces. You can see pride on their faces as everyone oohs and aahs. But you can also see discouragement in other moms who don't have the time, energy, or gumption to create such a thing.

My daughter has told me about the pelican-pretzel-tower treat, or the marshmallow-snowman-s'mores-fest someone else's mom brought into class. I could tell she was impressed and hoped I'd jump on that bandwagon. Somehow the store-bought cupcakes I'd brought to class months earlier now seemed lame. But honestly, those Pin-creations sound like a whole bunch of work to me. Maybe you're one of the gifted who can pull off the most amazing handiwork; I'm not.

Sometimes I feel guilty for not finding the time to delight my daughter with creative snacks like those other moms. I'm super challenged in the baking department to begin with, so I'd rather shave my eyebrows than compete in that arena. But pressure to keep up with the latest and greatest Pinterest creations has resulted in a new tangle of guilt for us. Like we needed another social media outlet to remind us we're falling short of perfection.

What about other women in your same line of business or ministry whose online following skyrockets while yours barely makes it off the ground? You cyber-stalk and secretly watch her every move in hopes of discovering the secret to her success. But when your growth doesn't match hers, you feel hopeless. *Does anyone see me? Isn't my work/ministry important?* It seems no matter what you do, you'll never measure up to her.

Sometimes we try to satisfy our need to feel *good enough* by exaggerating to our online community. How would they know the truth anyway, right? If we want to be known as exciting and adventurous or charitable and generous, we'll update our status to represent that. Our marriage might be falling apart, but the photos we share make it look as if the honeymoon never ended. Maybe we are in a season of rough parenting, but our online updates put us in the running for mom of the year. Bankruptcy might be inevitable, but we brag about our latest purchase or upcoming vacation. We may crave being a stay-at-home mom, but our online community is sure we love climbing the corporate ladder.

The truth is, our day-to-day routine can often become mundane. We get bored with our jobs and jealous of others who travel to far-away places. Our kids zap all our energy and we dream of putting "free to a good home" signs around their necks and sitting them at the curb. Our husbands never seem to give us what we need. We want a new haircut or color and our wardrobe feels blasé. So we spice things up a bit, stretching the truth or flat out lying so our lives look just as exhilarating and fulfilling as everyone else's. We battle feelings of inferiority by presenting a different "me" to our online community.

How can we compete with updates such as, "I have the best husband in the world!" or "I love being a mom every second of every day," or "My life couldn't be more perfect!" or even, "I did it! I just got promoted to director in five short months!" Are you kidding me? No wonder we exaggerate about our lives. How can the average Joe compete with statuses like that? In a desperate move to feel special, we lie.

Self-promotion has become a huge tangle. We believe the better we appear to be, the better we will be. Our "Yay me!" campaign is an attempt to silence the *not good enough* messages that whisper in our ears. And since it's all online, reaching to the ends of the earth, who would know if we're really advertising the truth? Very few.

So we market ourselves as having a charmed life. We boast about our grand adventures on vacations. We show off the kids, feigning humility as we crow about their achievements. We toot our own horn with career successes. Are we feeling better yet? We want others to think our husbands and kids are blessed to have us. And as we share Scripture online, we hope others will see just how very holy we are. Social media has left us desperate to feel good about who we are and determined to make others envious of the lives we lead.

⁓ ℓ ⌀

Don't get me wrong, there's a part of social media I love! You can post one little success or challenge and your entire tribe will know about it. That beats sharing via phone calls and emails any day. It's fun to see what others are up to and look at pictures of growing families. We can keep track of our friends across the country with a few clicks of the mouse. We learn about milestones, celebrations, losses, and needs while sitting in our favorite chair. The web gives us instant connection to those we love and helps us keep up with old and new friends. For that, I'm a huge fan of social media. But when it's used as a tool to elevate ourselves, I'm not a fan at all.

Proverbs 27:2 says, "Don't praise yourself; let others do it!" (TLB). Ouch, right? There's a very fine line to walk here. Just how do we share the good things that have happened without praising ourselves? Let's think about it.

God gave us talent, but we had to develop it. God blessed us financially, but we had to be good stewards. He has opened and closed doors, but we had to faithfully obey his prompting. So we have participated in our successes. It took our time and effort. But our self-worth gets tangled when we take all the credit, forgetting that it all started with God.

We can gush-brag, when we sing our own praises loudly. It might look like this: "Oh my, I am amazing! I just ran this marathon twenty minutes faster than my last marathon!" We can also humble-brag. We convey the same level of excitement but make it appear unassuming. "Wow, pinch me. I just shook Oprah's hand at a $1,000-a-plate charity dinner." Either way, it does something for us. There's a payoff. When our bragging works and the online community oohs and aahs our updates, we feel better about ourselves. We get the adoration and affirmation we wanted. And God has no part in it.

In 2 Corinthians 11:30, Paul challenges our thinking. "But if I must brag, I would rather brag about the things that show how weak I am" (TLB). Come again? Do you know anyone online (or in person for that matter) who brags about their deficiencies? Me, either—at least not often. But I appreciate Paul's words and his call to shift our posture in what we share.

When he tells us to brag about weakness, he's not suggesting we self-deprecate. We don't need to list all the ways we fall short. What Paul is asking us to do is recognize God's role in our lives. When we give up control and recognize our human-sized limitations, God's graciousness, faithfulness, and provision shine through us. Others will know he is the wellspring of our gifts and talents—both of which need our participation to bloom.

For this book to make it into your hands, I've had to hone my craft. God prompted me to start blogging many years ago and I obeyed. He opened doors for me to blog for other ministries and I accepted. He stirred me to self-publish and I found the support team to make it happen. And because I continued to say yes to him, he opened the door to write this book—a message I was born to share. Without him, I wouldn't have had words to fill these pages.

I can't brag about getting a book deal but I can boast that he blessed me with it. I'm not going to talk about my writing abilities but I will acknowledge he gave them to me. I cannot take credit for surviving the hard times I've shared in this book but I can brag that he steadied me. God gave me courage to be vulnerable even though I struggle with insecurity. He gave me the vision to write the things I've shared with you. And while I've had to be obedient and say yes, the fruit of my life stems from him. Yours does too.

You know what else this shift in perspective does? It untangles us from striving for significance and acceptance with our online community. We understand that our self-worth isn't dependent on the adoration of the world. Truth is, we're nothing without Jesus. And when we say yes to him, he will bless every part of our lives. Now that's something to brag about.

Social Media's Manipulations

Growing up, I didn't have instant access to the world like we do now. I didn't have email. My phone wasn't smart. A status update was when you dated someone more popular than yourself. Tweeting was the sound a bird made. Pinning meant you wrote something down on paper and stuck it on a tack board. And social media was playing my records at a basement party. Being able to connect to the world with just a click of a mouse is a newfound and much-welcomed freedom. I'm sure some of you are laughing because you've never known life to be any different.

Regardless, we're learning how to navigate our online presence with integrity and where the boundaries of healthy interactions lie. We're figuring out how much of our lives to share, and paying the consequences for making bad choices. But more than anything, we're facing a new tangle opportunity for our self-esteem.

My ministry is 90 percent online. I'm constantly connecting with women from all walks of life, all around the world. Social media has opened new doors that would otherwise be closed, and for that I love it. But it's also been a huge source of discouragement and frustration. When my agent was shopping this book around to different publishing houses, it seemed as though everyone else and their dog were getting book deals. But not me.

I'd see pictures of my friends signing their contracts, big smiles across their faces. There were posts about their struggles to meet writing deadlines. Many shared their word count woes. And when newly printed books arrived, they shared it online and received congratulations in the comments. I wanted to celebrate with my friends. Their accomplishments were worthy of praise. But every time I logged on and read their updates, I logged off feeling defeated. It tangled me up in *not good enough* feelings.

What was wrong with my writing? Wasn't my story worth telling? When would it be my turn? (Of course extra whip and caramel drizzle on my Frappuccino helped, but that was a temporary [and expensive] fix.) I wanted validation like others in my online community had received. And when it didn't come, it tightened the tangle that said I was worthless. Instead of trusting God's timing, I threw temper tantrums and pity parties. Super unattractive.

But when my publishing contract finally came, I never announced it online. Isn't that interesting? My story had finally been accepted for print, something I'd envied in others for over a year, and I couldn't share it online. If I had, it would have been for the wrong reasons and I knew it. It would have been an attempt to publically redeem my failure—a way to boost my self-worth and show others I was good enough. God whispered into my spirit, *You don't need to prove a thing.*

Social media has an uncanny way of exposing our insecurities, doesn't it? It triggers those *not good enough* messages like nobody's business.

You'll Be Good Enough When . . .

This message is a reminder your worth is dependent on your performance. You'll receive your *good enough* stamp of approval just as soon as what needs to happen does. It might look like this:

When you lose the weight, then you'll be as attractive as her.

When you get promoted at work, then you'll be as successful as her.

When you renovate your home, then you'll be able to entertain and impress like she does.

When you go organic or holistic, then you'll be a good mom like her.

You're Good Enough Because . . .

This message says you've done something right—that your efforts are paying off. It encourages you to keep working so you can live in the glow of "good-enough-dom." Do any of these ring a bell?

You should feel important because *she* accepted your friend request.

Your plan worked because you now have *this* number of followers.

Your wisdom is notable because the content you create gets shared a lot.

You'll Be Good Enough If . . .

This message says specific things have to exist before you're considered worthy in the eyes of others.

You have to develop relevant content.

You must constantly promote yourself.

Your online persona must be a certain way (happy, funny, insightful, and so on).

You must emulate her style.

Talk about keeping us on the treadmill of performance! We're working ourselves to the bone looking for acceptance and it's bankrupting our self-worth.

Ditch Those Unhealthy Habits

According to an article titled "Why Women Constantly Lie about Life on Facebook," at least one in four women admitted to lying or enhancing their updates between one and three times a month.[1] Even scarier, almost one in ten said they lied several times a week. Why? The report cites three reasons:

They were afraid their lives would seem boring.

They were jealous of others' status updates.

They wanted to impress friends and followers.

"We work very hard presenting ourselves to the world online, pretending and attempting to be happy all the time which is exhausting and ultimately unfulfilling," said Dr. Michael Sinclair, a leading British psychologist.[2]

When I did an internet search on the effects social media has on a woman's self-esteem, I quickly found more than enough material to prove my point. From clinical depression to extreme anxiety to struggles with worthlessness, the effects of a social media–based self-esteem are taking their toll. Although we may present a happy cyber-life, the truth is we're unhappy with who we are. We're certain that being more like *her* will change it all.

Ephesians 5:1 tells us to "imitate God like dearly loved children" (CEB), learning how Jesus lived on earth and trying to be like him in our day-to-day journey. Jesus knew who he was and made no apologies for it. He loved and celebrated others rather than being jealous of them. Christ was honest about his life rather than inflating it to impress those who followed him. He was the Son of God yet walked the earth a humble servant. Jesus is the only one we should imitate and his approval is all we should want.

What if we decided to stop trying to impress our online community and instead pointed others to God with the things we share? What if we showed wisdom and discernment in how much and what we shared? What if we stopped measuring our worth through our social media numbers? What if we celebrated others instead of comparing ourselves to them? Sounds wonderful, right? With that in mind, I'd like to suggest several social media habits that keep us from making those things a reality.

Sharing the Details of Our Weight Loss Journey

This has always perplexed me. I've never been able to find any good reason to offer such personal details for the world's consumption. I know some justify it, thinking it will help with accountability, but isn't that what private messages and local friends are for?

Some of you might have good reasons for sharing your weight loss journey on social media. I don't have the final or definitive word on it. But I would encourage you to ask yourself what the motives behind it are. Are you looking for applause? Are you seeking approval? Are you trying to please the world?

In the end, though, it's between you and God.

Talking about Our Time of the Month

While this seems to be a given, I've seen my fair share of women discuss their menstrual cycle on social media. It's acceptable to share when you're out with the girls, but it's not okay to inform the online world that Aunt Flo has come to visit. Seriously.

As a teenager I had horrible cramps. When they'd wake me in the middle of the night, I'd creep into my parents' room to get my mom. Don't we always want our moms when we don't feel good? She'd get me medicine and a heating pad and tuck me back into bed. One night as I opened their door, my dad sat straight up in bed and said, "Can't you handle your period on your own?"

I guess it really was my issue to deal with, and we laugh about it now, but his words made me realize I didn't need to involve others. I'm giving you the same advice. Handle it alone, girls. You don't need to garner cyber-sympathy.

Boasting about Our Good Deeds

I have a friend who posts every time she feeds the homeless or gives money to the needy. When she writes her monthly check to the Humane Society, everyone knows it. When she signs up for a missions trip, it ends up in my Facebook feed. When she buys a medicated net to protect sleeping children from malaria in Africa, I hear about it.

I appreciate that she wants to help others. I love her financial generosity. But when she boasts about it online, it's to overcompensate for *not good enough* feelings somewhere else. The Bible clearly tells us to use our resources to help others but not so our reputation benefits from it.

Tossing Out Teaser Phrases

What do you do when someone posts "Need prayer!" as their status update? You ask for more information, right? What about when someone posts "I've got news!"? Naturally, you want to know what it is.

Sometimes we feel unnoticed or unappreciated and we want a little attention. It happens. That's just life, right? But it becomes a tangle when we make statements like these hoping others will reach out to us for an answer.

It's manipulation, pure and simple. And often our worth is dependent on the number of responses we receive.

If you have news, by all means share it so we can celebrate with you! If you're bold enough to ask for prayer online, be specific so we know what to pray. But don't post teaser phrases to fill your need to be noticed.

Airing Our Complaints

I'm always amazed by how negative we can be. Do you know women who complain about all their struggles online? Are you one of them?

They share how their husband is insensitive, their kids are too high-maintenance, their bills are never-ending, their health is always failing, and the list goes on. They're searching for sympathy. It's a way for them to feel loved and supported, but it's not healthy.

We all have a battle (or two) we're fighting right now, but when we fill our Facebook feeds with the details we look needy.

I will certainly post things that drive me nuts—all in good humor—careful not to cross the line from cute to critical. As a rule, I am positive online, even when I've had a bad day. I recently posted this: "I don't like it when Tuesday feels like Monday. Wouldn't it be nice to have a full week of Fridays?" That's about as negative as I'll get.

Use wisdom in how and what you share, and check your motives. The teacher may have been irrational and the bill collector rude, but your online community isn't your therapist. And going to them rather than to God for validation and sympathy is a dangerous tangle.

Making Rude and Judgmental Comments

The Enemy has done a fabulous job of pitting women against one another. Rather than stand together in support, we're quick to tear each other down. And we're doing it on social media.

Being a mom with a tweener daughter, I'm concerned with how culture and media affect my girl. Hollywood doesn't give me a lot to work with, you know? But one of our favorite celebrities is former Disney star Demi Lovato. Yep, I love her just as much as Sara does.

She's walked a difficult road of healing with struggles such as cutting and an eating disorder, but she has emerged as a strong voice of reason. Among other things, she's taking on the issue of cyber-bullying, and I applaud her for standing up and speaking out.

After a recent awards show, someone tweeted that Lovato's arms looked "fat" in her dress. It's beyond me why anyone would feel the need to slam a sister, but this young girl did. And Demi's response was perfect. She said, "Who cares?"

When we judge other women publically like that, it gives us a false sense of superiority. It may temporarily boost our self-worth, but to others we look shallow and mean-spirited. Talk about a tricky tangle!

165

What if instead we linked arms as a gender and refused to have any part in knotting each other's self-worth? Rather than judge, what if we looked for the best in each other? Instead of pointing out flaws, what if we were the ones saying, "Who cares?" The World Wide Web is tangled up enough. Let's not add to it.

Let these truths sink in today.

You are not the sum of your social media stats.

Because of Jesus, your worth can't be measured by comments, followers, or likes.

God made you on purpose, so don't try to look different online.

If someone's online life looks too good to be true, it probably is.

You don't have to exaggerate your life to make others like you.

Sweet one, you're so much more than those things.

You are the world's seasoning, to make it tolerable. If you lose your flavor, what will happen to the world? And you yourselves will be thrown out and trampled underfoot as worthless. You are the world's light—a city on a hill, glowing in the night for all to see. Don't hide your light! Let it shine for all; let your good deeds glow for all to see, so that they will praise your heavenly Father. (Matt. 5:13–16 TLB)

You flavor the world. You illumine it with your kindness. And you have the privilege of using both salt and light to point others to God.

Her Tangle: A Story from Shanyn

Do you have any experience with barbed wire? I do. I'm a farm girl, and I've grown up surrounded by it. It's a wicked thing, really. Something man invented both for animals and for war. Typically it is a twisted pair of wires with sharp barbs woven in. They grab. They cut. They don't let go easily. They maim. They can kill.

For so many, social media—our blogs, Facebook pages, Twitter feeds, Instagram, Pinterest—can be the barbed wire that snarls us.

I remember a time I got tangled up, cut and bleeding. I was invited to be a part of an online ministry and was very excited. It was with women I admired, and I liked them very much. We were collaborating on something that would powerfully minister to other women.

And in the name of collaboration, I enthusiastically offered the talents, skills, and passions God had blessed me with. I was innocently trying to help—to make the ministry more effective. But I made a critical error. I got caught up in serving the ministry itself rather than serving God.

My heart was in the right spot, but my efforts were completely misunderstood. The owner thought I was trying to take over—making a power play for the ministry. But in all honesty that had never crossed my mind. What came next stunned me.

In a group email and on social media, I was disciplined using Scripture as a backup. I was publically accused of sinful motives and game-playing, in front of women I admired. When private messages and emails came asking, "What is going on?" . . . I had no answer. I didn't have one to give.

I realize now that I was caught in the tangle of someone else's insecurity—her desire to be seen as a leader. But I got tangled up too. I was publically blamed for a crime I didn't commit and tagged as a troublemaker. It hurt.

Friends, it was horrible. I cried. I prayed. And I chose not to defend myself. While I washed my cuts in salty tears, God washed them in grace. Deciding to let him untangle the barbs instead of struggling against them was hard, but I needed his precision.

As I walked away from the situation—cutting ties with the ministry—I began to pray for them. I forgave her for the online humiliation. And rather than fight the barbed wire that dug into my self-worth, I surrendered the relationship to God.

Social media can be a big tangle. On one hand, we try to keep everyone happy, posting the things that fit with the majority. We stay safe with our words instead of speaking about hard stuff. We are too insecure to write about the real, the dirty, the messy—the stuff that isn't pretty.

On the other hand, we try to impress. We want others to think we know God's Word so well. We look for the hits, the comments, the shares, the "Wow, you know your stuff!" affirmations. But deep down, we fear judgment, failure, controversy, arguments, confrontations, and the occasional war in our blog comments following what should have been an encouraging post.

Sometimes we look for others to help us untangle from the social media barbs, but their best intentions can't free us. But when we write and share for an audience of One, the barbs lose their power to dig into our hearts.

It's important that my online and offline persons align. I want others to know I love Jesus in my home, at the store, at church, and online. I ask myself this question everyday: *If the words I tweet, blog, and use in my status updates were shared anonymously, would others know my faith from them?*

I had an acquaintance message me a while back. She had visited my blogs but had never commented on a post. She hadn't shared them on Facebook or Twitter. But she wanted me to know that she reads them. Sometimes she emails them or prints them out. And she wanted to ask for prayer.

It had zero to do with me and *everything* to do with Jesus. She saw him in my words and in my life, and that blessed me beyond measure. It's times like this that make me thankful for social media.

But beware the barbs associated with it. Even today, when I see posts from that group, or that person who publically humiliated me, it still stings a bit. I'm human. I grieve over a misunderstanding that got out of control in the faceless, voiceless confines of social media. When you can't see a face, hear a voice, or touch a hand, you lose some ability to reach the heart of another person.

～ Shanyn

His Anchor

What this adds up to, then, is this: no more lies, no more pretense. Tell your neighbor the truth. In Christ's body we're all connected to each other, after all. When you lie to others, you end up lying to yourself. (Eph. 4:25)

> Truth lasts;
> lies are here today, gone tomorrow. (Prov. 12:19)

Whenever you're trying to look better than others or get the better of others, things fall apart and everyone ends up at the others' throats. (James 3:16)

Your Untangling Prayer

Lord, I confess I'm tangled in the web of social media. I've allowed my self-worth to be defined by the number of followers, fans, likes, retweets, or repins I have in my circle of influence. I've exaggerated my life and my circumstances to impress others, trying to make my life look better or different. I've fallen into the comparison trap, sometimes feeling inferior and other times superior. It's made me insecure in who I am.

Would you untie all the online places where I am knotted up with insecurity and anchor my self-esteem in Jesus instead? I don't want to satisfy my need to feel valuable through my online community. It was never meant to take your place. I'm sorry for giving social media more power in my life than I've given you. It's become an idol, and I have allowed it to meet a need only you can truly meet. Please forgive me.

I need your help to loosen the tangle. I can't do this without you, Father. Help me to never again look for love and acceptance through Facebook, Twitter, Pinterest, or the like, and give me wisdom to know when I'm headed for a snarl.

In all the ways I connect online, please bless my heart's desire to imitate Christ. Let me be a light in the social media world, always pointing back to you.

Thank you that in your eyes, I'm good enough just the way I am.

In the name of Jesus. Amen.

Loosening the Knot Questions

1. How has your self-worth been positively or negatively affected by social media?

2. When you see the status updates of others, what emotions are stirred inside you? How do you respond?

3. Have you ever embellished an update? How did it make you feel? How long did that feeling last?

4. How do you need to change your social media habits and hang-ups?

5. What is the Holy Spirit speaking to you right now?

Tangled in the Snare of Success

I've worked most of my life. Both of my parents had demanding jobs and modeled a strong work ethic that rubbed off on me. I enjoy contributing to the world, and my working career started when I was very young.

Like many young girls I was a babysitter, and that was a job I did only for the money. I'm not made to take care of other people's children. While kids love me, they make me nervous. And I sweat. I have several friends who work at a preschool, and whenever they need a substitute they giggle and suggest the director call me. Some women might take offense and end up with hurt feelings, but not me. I adore my kids and love my friends' children, but I am not Mary Poppins to those littles I don't know. It's just a cold hard fact.

My first legitimate job was answering phones at a pizza joint. I gained weight at this job for obvious reasons, but I enjoyed the people and the social aspect of it. I moved from there to a short-lived hostess position at a local restaurant. When that closed a few months later, I was hired to make change at a large amusement park's outside arcade area, wearing a brown polyester uniform that had no figure-flattering abilities. In the summers I taught tennis, a job I loved. I also did grunt work as an office assistant, and even sold encyclopedias over the phone.

As I look back, these jobs were just . . . jobs. I didn't find my self-worth in them. My identity wasn't wrapped up in how much I made or the company I worked for. There was little stress and lots of fun. I'd go to work, do what I was hired to do, punch out at the end of the day, and then go live my life. These seasonal and temporary jobs didn't define who I was but rather what I did to earn money. It was tangle-free. In college, though, my perspective shifted.

During my last few years, I worked at a local advertising agency. It started as an internship and eventually turned into a paid position. This was the first job where I felt a sense of satisfaction. The owner of the firm saw value in my free work, enough to employ me part-time. And while I was quite the poster child for bad choices in college, I never did anything to jeopardize this job.

I took pride in my work and ownership in my position. It suppressed a place in me that felt my best was never good enough. Even as I write this, I'm overwhelmed with gratitude. I realize now how very much I needed the owner's affirmation back then. I hadn't made that connection until now.

Once I graduated, I drove back to my childhood home, certain a fantastic job was right around the corner. But it wasn't. I assured Mom and Dad I'd only be home for a few months, but it took a year. I felt defeated. I'd left college confident in my education and experience, but those familiar *not good enough* feelings crept back in with a vengeance. *Why doesn't any employer see my value? What's wrong with me?*

This is where the tangle began. Most of my friends had jobs before they graduated, and I moved back home with my parents.

That wasn't exactly what I had in mind. Eventually I landed my first post-college job, but it wasn't enough money to enable me to afford an apartment.

Promotions happened. New jobs came along. And eventually I was able to step out on my own. I began to thrive. That's what a good job and success can do to you.

Success is very important to us. It's the common American model, and we take great pride in our ability to do a job well. When we meet someone new, our work is usually one of the first things we share about ourselves, and one of the first pieces of information we want to know about them. While our jobs may help to define us, we get tangled when we let them measure our worth in the world.

For example, it's fair to say that I'm a Jesus freak. Let's just call a spade a spade. And my job is to shine his light in the world. I'm also a mom to Sam and Sara, and it's one of the most rewarding (and one of the hardest) roles I've had the privilege of playing. God blessed me with my husband, Wayne, and I love being his wife, even when he is super annoying.

I've worked in the nonprofit sector for most of my career because I appreciate serving the *least of these*. God has trusted me with a ministry that speaks his truth into the weary self-esteem of women, and I am grateful for every opportunity it affords me. I value these jobs that define me, just as I should. But when I anchor my self-worth in their success or failure, I get knotted up.

It's normal to want success in life. There's nothing wrong in desiring to be a contributing member of society. There are few things better than feeling a sense of satisfaction from your job. Meaningful work goes a long way in making you emotionally healthy and happy. God gave us brilliant minds and aspirations to make a difference. He blessed us with talents and creativity so we could express ourselves. He gave us a heart to help others in need.

But sometimes we define ourselves by success in what we do instead of factoring in who we are. Rather than secure our self-esteem in Jesus, we allow it to fluctuate based on how we perform in our work. Instead of believing we're worthy no matter the career we have or the job we're doing, we buy into the lie that our worth is based on our success or failure. If we *do* good, then we *are* good. And if so, then the opposite must also be true. It's a tricky knot.

I'm not advocating we shouldn't strive to be good at what we do. We should certainly work toward excellence. God demonstrates that in the creation story. I'm not suggesting that furthering our education is frivolous. He gave us a mind and delights when we use it. It shows integrity when we want to do a good job and be effective in our work. And being rewarded for a job well done is one of the best feelings on earth. We just can't let these achievements and accomplishments serve as measuring sticks for our self-worth. And there are lots of ways our self-worth can become tangled up in success.

The Tangle of Failure

Because the world tells us we should, we put pressure on ourselves to do it all. And we can—at least for a while. We function in many roles with high expectations, but eventually we will fall short somewhere. Our Wonder Woman capabilities break down, letting others see that we're merely human. And rather than give ourselves grace, we label ourselves a *failure*.

You may feel you're not being a good steward of the calling God has placed on your life. And the fear of failing him overwhelms you. I get that. God never asks us to do things that are super easy, and it's intimidating to put yourself in a situation where you might fail. Or, perhaps worse, look stupid.

When I knew God wanted me to speak to groups of women, I freaked out. Back in the day I was a nervous face-sweater. Within minutes, mascara would be running into my eyes and burning like crazy. You know exactly how that feels.

174

I'm sure those in the first few rows thought I had an anxiety-induced eye twitch. Yes, it was that noticeable. Every time I'd step off the stage, I was sure people would ask for their money back. I just knew I'd let everyone down, including God. But the speaking invitations kept coming, I continued to say yes, and my friends reminded me that waterproof mascara had been invented.

We might feel like a disappointment because we don't bring in enough money to support our family the way we'd like. When we have to say no to travel baseball or summer camp or those new shoes because the funds aren't there, the tangle of failure tightens. We wonder why we can't make more money—why we aren't more of a financial success.

In a business world that rewards achievement instead of effort, we're afraid to fail. In our minds, failing translates to *failure.* So anything less than perfect means we're not good enough. We struggle to separate the work from the person. And when we can't, it tangles our self-worth.

It might look like this:

If you disappoint your boss or fall short of your quota, you're worthless.

If you try a new venture and fail, you're a flop.

If others don't value your work, you're a disappointment.

If you don't deliver perfection, you've wasted their time and money.

If your project doesn't stand above the rest, you're nothing but average.

But I once heard somone say that failure is trying to please everyone, all the time. And sometimes that everyone is us. We can be our own worst critic.

It's not only in the workplace. We can struggle with failure as a stay-at-home mom too. Just the other night, I had to order in pizza. I had thawed ground beef to make spaghetti, but there wasn't sauce in the pantry. So I decided to make sloppy joes instead, but we were out of ketchup. I finally reached for the taco seasoning packet, but it wasn't there. I couldn't even keep up with the groceries, for heaven's sake.

Or I remember the time my husband needed a pair of pants from the cleaners for a business trip, and I forgot to pick them up in time. I've over-promised to my kids and let them down. I've missed bill payments. I've left dairy-fresh milk in the cooler on the porch all day in the hot sun. And the list goes on.

As homemakers, we can experience just as much failure as those who sit in offices all day. While it may look different, it's disappointment just the same. And it leaves us feeling worthless.

I wish we could truly understand that letting anyone or anything other than God decide our worth will crush us. Our self-worth shouldn't be determined by our performance, because it's already been determined by our Creator.

The Tangle of Age

I used to have a mind of steel and could remember every detail of every single thing. But after kids, that changed. I contracted mommy-brain, a condition that sucks memory capabilities out of existence. I was sure the effects would reverse as my kids grew and started thinking for themselves, but I was wrong. And with their schedules busier than ever before, my poor brain is taxed.

I've noticed that tasks and meetings are more apt to slip off my radar. My days are packed with important things that I can't afford to forget. So I've enlisted the help of an online calendar. It's the only thing that keeps me on-task these days. If you were to look at it, you'd see prompts to phone a friend, pay a bill, or some other random reminder. It's my key to successfully running life with a forty-plus brain.

When I forget something for my family, my job, or my ministry, I beat myself up about it. I remember the days my brain worked at full capacity—it was a glorious thing. I miss it. Knowing age is a culprit triggers messages that tell me I'm not as good as I used to be. It says I'm letting people down. It strikes fear that I'll be replaced. I feel inadequate.

When those younger, sharper people walk into the office, it stirs up all sorts of worries. Your insecurities skyrocket, and fear you won't be able to keep up rears its ugly head. When the word you're looking for is hiding in your brain and you can't find it during a presentation, that's distressing. And your self-worth takes a hit.

We live in a world that glorifies youth. It's worshiped. It's revered. It's pursued. And we can't deny the reality that aging takes a physical and mental toll on our bodies. But neither of those things should make a hill of beans worth of difference in our value as women. While it may look different, there is success to be had at any age. But even that can't define our worth.

The Tangle of Comparison and Jealousy

It's easy to compare our work to the work of others. Being competitive is part of our DNA—at least on some level. It's natural to want to be the best, and for some of us there's no place we'd rather be. But wanting to be number one takes its toll on our worth.

I'll see a blog post come through my email that tangles me because the author has put into words what I've been struggling to write for the past week. Or I'll see a clever status update that gets lots of attention and I'll beat myself up for not thinking of it first.

I've shared the platform with speakers who engage the audience better than I do. I've seen book sales explode with an author-friend but remain a trickle for me. Sometimes I just don't feel good about my work when I compare it to hers. I bet you know exactly what I mean, because you've let someone else's success dwarf your own.

A few years ago, a friend challenged me to think differently. I was frustrated that my ministry wasn't growing as quickly as another's. She said, "Don't envy her success. You're not equipped to handle the blessings or the challenges that come with it." Ba-bam! What a timely word that proved to be.

We've all looked at the accomplishments of others and wanted to gag ourselves with a spoon, right? We've been critical, trying to discredit their work because that somehow makes us feel better about ours. The creativity and talents of others can annoy us because it just doesn't seem fair. Everything falls into their lap, and we're left wondering, *Why not me?*

Maybe we're the measuring stick for others and we delight in our position of power. We think we're all that and a bag of chips, and enjoy shining above the rest. Jealousy works in our favor, because we're the ones who come out on top. People want to be us. They want what we have. And our self-esteem rests on a false sense of superiority. (By the way, don't be like this. It isn't cool.)

What about when we see successful women who don't seek God in their work? Their business is booming while ours is inching along. It's deflating.

I know a woman who owns her own business. She's nice enough and tosses out God's name from time to time, but her lifestyle reeks of the world. Her kids are young and often unsupervised, and she opens her home to parties and questionable people all the time. She engages in activity that makes me blush (and I'm not a prude), and yet her wallet is busting at the seams.

Can I be honest? This drives me nuts. There are plenty of us who "play by the rules" and seek God's will for our lives. We try to be upstanding. We're generous with our money and time. We follow the path we feel God has laid out before us, yet our money trees are not blooming.

You know what I think? The Enemy doesn't need to exert much effort for the ones who don't seek God. He already has them. But he must work overtime to discourage a believer. And one of the ways is jealousy. We start lusting after their success. Then we read this verse: "No lusting after your neighbor's house—or wife or servant or maid or ox or donkey. Don't set your heart on anything that is your neighbor's" (Exod. 20:17).

I don't envy their house or spouse, and I don't covet their pets. But I am guilty of setting my heart on the ministry of another. I've envied a success or a victory. I've wished for her kind of results in my own work. Chances are, you have too.

This tangle happens when we forget to count our blessings and instead count hers.

The Tangle of Guilt

As women, we have a knack for feeling guilt over everything. Sweet mother. But when it comes to our work, this hits us right between the eyes.

Many of us have jobs outside the home. We find great joy in what we do, and a career isn't negotiable. Sometimes it's a necessity, and we work to help support our family financially. Regardless of the reason, it's common to feel that pang of guilt as we grab our keys and head out the door. We wonder if our kids will grow up to be well-adjusted if we're not around all day. We feel bad for not having a hot meal on the table when our husband comes home. We're frustrated the laundry is still piled up by the washing machine. And even if we love our work, we're guilt-ridden that we might be failing at home.

Others of us are stay-at-home moms. We manage the home and everyone's schedule. And while we work our tails off, we feel moments of guilt for not bringing home an actual paycheck. We might overcompensate with hot meals and clean homes, looking for visual reminders of our worth. It makes us feel better, like we're successfully contributing to the family. But we can't shake the guilt that says we're not doing enough. We get tangled in the lie that says only a 9 to 5 working woman is a valuable one.

Few things can tangle us more than guilt. It tells us no matter what we do or how hard we work, it's not good enough. We're a failure. And so often, guilt triggers a performance-based reaction that makes us work harder to prove our worth.

The Tangle of Approval

I want to do well, and sometimes I want others to notice. Okay, more than just sometimes. And I know I'm not alone on this one. As women, we have a deep need to be seen. It feels good when others appreciate our work. It validates something deep inside our wounded hearts.

When I write a blog post—really pour myself into it—and no one cares enough to leave a comment, it hurts. It often manifests as anger or a "who gives a rip" attitude. But the truth is I didn't write that post for kicks. I wrote it to get a response. And so often, that's exactly what tangles me.

God's been working this out in me. I'm trying to dissolve the expectation that others will notice and connect with me. I know God uses my words to help others. He uses yours too. But we may never have tangible evidence to prove it.

We might never hear the impact we've made as a teacher, a writer, a doctor, an office assistant, or a volunteer. There's a chance we won't get a pat on the back for a job well done. Our boss might not publicly recognize our hard work. The kids may never thank us for doing their laundry and our husbands might never know all the work we do to keep the home running smoothly.

If we do what we do hoping for approval or recognition, we're setting ourselves up for disappointment. When we allow the praise of others to define our worth or determine our success, we're tangled.

Colossians 3:23 says, "Whatever you do, work at it with all your heart, as though you were working for the Lord and not for people" (GNT). Simply put, we serve an audience of One. Working for the adoration of anyone else is a surefire way to knot up our self-worth.

The Tangle of Money

Self-worth and net worth have a complicated relationship. So often we think they are the same, but they're not. Self-worth is how we value ourselves, and net worth is the difference between what we own and what we owe. They're worlds apart.

The biggest expectation we have as we climb the ladder of success is seeing big dollar signs at the top. We want the fancy cars and the big houses that go along with our awesomeness, and money is the only way to get those things.

She has the expensive jog stroller we couldn't afford. Her cookware is top-of-the-line and costs more than our monthly food and entertainment budget combined. Her kids attend the expensive summer camps. And the list goes on.

In our minds, money is the key to happiness. And being successful is the only way to get it, so our focus becomes building our own kingdoms. In the end, we have a bloated self-image fueled by a fat bank account. But this will eventually leave us bankrupt.

First Timothy 6:10 explains why: "Certainly, the love of money is the root of all kinds of evil. Some people who have set their hearts on getting rich have wandered away from the Christian faith and have caused themselves a lot of grief" (GW). Money isn't the problem. But the love of it is.

That's where we get tangled. In the eyes of the divine, there isn't enough money in the world to increase our worth. But we try anyway.

The Tangle of Expectation

My passion is speaking to groups of women. I love it. There's something about being on stage, sharing how God has been big in a situation, and watching "aha" moments on women's faces. I get a kick out of seeing God's truth smack someone upside the head. And my heart breaks for the woman who sits in tears because she can relate to my story. I totally dig it.

While there are writers who end up speaking to support their books, I'm a speaker who has somehow found herself writing. My heart comes alive when I'm behind a microphone, not a computer screen. But for some reason, God has me here.

I knew something was up when the new year was around the corner and my speaking calendar was light. And by light, I mean it had nothing on it. I easily give over twenty talks a year at events ranging from weekend retreats to Christmas teas to local MOPS groups. It's been steady for many years now, and a full calendar is an expectation. But now it was empty instead.

Oh my stars, that triggered my *not good enough* messages like nobody's business. Had I done something wrong? Had I finally exhausted God? My ministry had been growing and I'd been successful in speaking and blogging, but for some reason everything had stopped. This wasn't how it was supposed to be.

It's easy to measure success by fulfilled expectations. But how do you define success when there's nothing to measure? Everything in me wanted to freak out, but God and I had been on a journey as of late. I'd been learning to trust him with my self-worth rather than listening to the world. And it paid off.

I was calm. Even months into the new year with nothing on the books, I waited for God to move. So when my agent called with news of a publishing contract, knowing it would take me the rest of the year to write and edit, it all made sense.

Had my speaking calendar been full, I might have missed book deadlines. I might have been distracted by my favored avenue of ministry. I may not have given my full attention to God and the words he wanted on these pages. I expected God to bless my ministry in the way I thought best, but he had other plans.

We each have expectations of what success looks like in our work, in our ministry, or in how we run our homes. And our self-worth can get tangled up when we don't reach them. Sometimes we stink at giving ourselves grace. When we hold too tightly to what we think should happen, it sets us up to feel like a failure. Because more times than not, God's plans are different. Better. Untangling our worth from our expectations means we move forward with the plans we've made but adjust quickly when we see God changing them up.

There are countless ways we let the pursuit of success knot us up. But at the root there's a common thread. We expect the work we do—be it inside or outside the home—to help determine the value we hold as women. We tangle our self-worth in achievements and accomplishments. And we measure our significance in dollar signs.

But God measures success differently. He looks at our obedience and faithfulness. He watches our willingness to walk out his purpose for our lives. He looks for humility instead of pride. And when we begin to measure our success by these things, our tangles will begin to fall free.

Her Tangle: A Story from Julie

Ever felt forgotten by God? Ever wondered if you weren't "special" in his eyes anymore? You've done amazing stuff with him—all this great life or career or ministry stuff. You've known his presence and his workings in your life. You've been passionately committed and connected to your calling and you knew exactly what your life was about. And then out of nowhere, circumstances came along that changed every last drop of it.

All your dreams, all your passions, all that special stuff has been snuffed out and you're left feeling ordinary. You're empty inside, like nothing significant is happening in your life. And you're certain God has deleted your number.

Ever felt forgotten by God? I did.

A few years ago, my husband and I were in the thick of student ministry. We'd gotten married a couple years prior, and had both come into the marriage with a huge passion for working with high school students. At the time he was on staff at our church. And while he was the one with the official "pastor" title, I completely dove in beside him. I loved every drop of it.

I loved my girls, loved our big Sunday night events, loved our small midweek gatherings in our home. I lived and breathed student ministry, and knew this was exactly where I was meant to be. But then everything flipped upside down and my circumstances spun me completely around.

My father-in-law, who lived across the country, had progressive cancer. We began to wonder if we needed to live closer to him. Within the same breath, my husband got an out-of-the-blue job offer at a church thirty minutes from his parents' home. And after much prayer, we knew God was asking us to move.

So we did. We moved, and it was as crazy as moving can be. However, what I haven't shared yet is that two months prior to our move we adopted and brought home our two little boys from Haiti. We went from one to three kids in a matter of moments. I was suddenly a mom of multiple children, ages almost two, barely two, and right at three. Oh, yes, you can imagine.

It was chaotic. All I'd known was completely shaken like a snow globe, pieces and parts of my life swirling around without rhyme or reason. And when the whirlwind died down, I looked at my new life and wondered what in the world had just happened.

I wanted things to be normal again. I tried to re-engage with student ministry, but it all felt different, like an uncomfortable sweater that didn't fit right. Nothing was the same. And while

I had prayed like crazy to be a mom, something I desperately wanted, I had no idea what I was doing. I felt like I was drowning.

Sunday nights were the most difficult. While my husband prepped for the student service, I fed the kids. And instead of going to church with him, I watched him walk out the door without me. My heart would scream, *I want to go. I'm supposed to go! I'm called to student ministry too!* But everything had changed.

Sunday nights at our previous church were what I had lived for. So much intentional ministry happened with some of my favorite people on the planet. I got to engage from the front lines, watching teenage girls awaken to the call of God on their lives. In a matter of a few short months, I felt as though my identity was gone.

Student ministry was what I knew to my very core. For over fifteen years, it's where I gave my time and energy. It's what I scheduled my priorities around. It was my life. I wasn't seeking notoriety or fortune and fame; I genuinely loved the Lord and knew this was what I'd been created to do. How could it just disappear? But it did.

One might say, "You adopted from a foreign country, and adjustments needed to be made." But in the thick of it, it didn't feel like an *adjustment*. It felt like the shattering of a calling—a calling I'd lived in and loved with all my heart.

What do you do when your identity is shaken? How do you function when the way you've always done life is no longer an option?

You see, I had put a whole bunch of stock in my identity as "student ministry leader." And when I was no longer that, I grieved deeply. I felt lost and forgotten. Life suddenly felt small and insignificant. I wondered if I'd done something wrong, or if God no longer needed me.

The truth, however, was that my Savior had not forgotten me. He knew exactly what he was doing. God was right in the middle of my heartbreak, getting ready to move in powerful ways. Through his kindness, he directed me to Psalm 5:3, which says, "In the morning, O Lord, You will hear my voice; In the morning I will order my prayer to You and eagerly watch" (NASB).

As this verse leapt off the page one morning, here's what the Lord spoke to my heart.

He wants to hear my voice.

Few things are sweeter than when your little one curls up in your lap and says "Good morning, Mom." I realized God wanted to hear my voice too. How special and amazing that my God would want to hear me speak. How incredibly affirming.

He wants to hear my heart.

And first thing! Before the day kicks in, God wants me to bring him my thoughts, my dreams, my burdens, and my hopes. He doesn't want me walking into my day with more on my shoulders than I was ever meant to bear. How special and amazing that my God would want to carry my burdens. What compassion.

I need to anticipate that he will indeed move.

In this, God asks me to do something most interesting: watch eagerly. It implies I should expect something to happen. It reminds me that God is on the move and I should live in expectation. How special and amazing that my God is at work in me and around me.

These words poured truth into my weary soul. Even with my life being turned upside down, God was still moving. Even though my identity had changed, he had not. He was still faithful. He still had plans for me. And his work in my heart was intentional. That truth freed me.

So I began to watch. I began to believe once again. God stirred me with sweet expectation. And while I didn't see his hand immediately, I waited with hope.

In his time and at just the right moment, I saw God throw open doors. He untangled catastrophic knots. He miraculously orchestrated beautiful and tragic events. All in a way I could have never imagined. And though I'd been certain we'd never be biological parents, I became pregnant with our fourth child.

Years prior, I'd promised God that if he ever allowed me to carry a son, I would name him Zachary. I could have never known that my little boy would become my Ebenezer for this incredible season.

Zachary means "God remembered."

Ever feel forgotten by God? You're not, sweet friend. No matter where life may have you right now, God is moving. Whether you're in the middle of living out your calling, or the middle of all your questions and heartache, he sees you.

God wants to hear your voice. He wants to hear your dreams, your hurts, and your desires. And he wants you to watch eagerly, for he is indeed on the move.

"For I am confident of this very thing, that he who began a good work in you will perfect it until the day of Christ Jesus" (Phil. 1:6 NASB).

~Julie

───── ϵ⳽ His Anchor ↷ ─────

Commit your work to the Lord, then it will succeed. (Prov. 16:3 TLB)

Then I took a good look at everything I'd done, looked at all the sweat and hard work. But when I looked, I saw nothing but smoke. Smoke and spitting into the wind. There was nothing to any of it. Nothing. (Eccles. 2:11)

Will you gain anything if you win the whole world but lose your life? Of course not! There is nothing you can give to regain your life. (Matt. 16:26 GNT)

He who loves money shall never have enough. The foolishness of thinking that wealth brings happiness! (Eccles. 5:10 TLB)

───── ϵ⳽ Your Untangling Prayer ↷ ─────

Lord, my self-worth is tangled in my success. Needing to be seen by others and recognized for a job well done carries too much weight. It's not healthy, and I need your help to loosen the knot.

Would you remove the guilt? It seems no matter what I choose—be it work in the home or out—I feel like I'm letting others down. I need your confirmation that I am walking the path you've chosen.

I'm struggling with jealousy too. It seems _____ always outperforms me. I'm frustrated that I even compare myself to others, because it keeps me from seeing my own talents and gifts. Would you remind me I was made on purpose, with a different skillset than anyone else?

And Lord, give me confidence to do my work well. Help me remember that in all I do, I'm working for the approval of One. When I have that mindset, everything else will fall into place.

Let me trust you with the plans you have for my life. Help me define success based on my faithfulness and obedience to you. And when it seems you've forgotten me, help me trust you while I wait. I know you're always working behind the scenes.

Forgive me for seeking the world's affirmations above yours. And thank you for giving me the ability to contribute to my family, the community, and to the world.

In the name of Jesus. Amen.

Loosening the Knot Questions

1. Growing up, what kind of connection between work and self-worth did your family model?

2. How does success in your work positively or negatively affect how you feel about yourself?

3. What tangle do you identify with the most, and why? How can you change it?

4. What is the Holy Spirit speaking to you right now?

10

The Divine *Untangling*

It completely caught me off-guard. Did I hear God right? With all of the ministry outreach I do online, certainly he did not just ask me to fast from social media and blogging for the month of July—a month with thirty-one days to boot! It almost seemed unthinkable, but it was exactly what God had in mind.

I'd been at a weekend conference, listening to one of my favorite speakers. It didn't take long for God to get all up in my business. You know what I mean, right? Those times when the proverbial spotlight seems to call you out of the crowd, and you're certain the speaker is talking directly to you—and everyone else knows it. Well, it was one of those times. She said a simple phrase that hit me square between the eyes.

"Don't let your giftedness exceed your godliness." Spotlight. And even more, she shared this little nugget at the beginning of the weekend. I slowly slouched down into my seat, wrecked at the realization that this was exactly what I had been doing. It was going to be a long weekend.

When God thought each of us up, he handpicked our unique skills and talents. The plan was for us to use them to glorify him. But so often, we use those gifts for our benefit instead. We tangle them up in our relentless pursuit of feeling *good enough*. When others validate our abilities, we begin to crave their approval. Our actions get noticed, making us work harder to impress. We know God gave us the talent, but we believe the lie that says we have to work for recognition. And so we do.

Maybe you're an amazing singer or dancer. You might have the gift of gab or the ability to beautifully string words together on the page. Your heart may be filled with compassion or your mind with great wisdom. Regardless, God created you with special gifts to help you walk out the purpose he placed on your life. Ephesians 2:10 confirms this: "We are God's accomplishment, created in Christ Jesus to do good things. God planned for these good things to be the way that we live our lives" (CEB).

But here's where we get tangled. We take those *good things* and use them as measurements of our worth. We compare ourselves to others, looking to see who is better, prettier, wiser, faster—and the list goes on. Rather than love who God made us to be and understand the Creator intends each of us to be different, we step onto the performance-based treadmill and run ourselves into exhaustion trying to be as good as, if not better than, everyone else.

Psalm 46:10 says, "Cease striving and know that I am God" (NASB). This verse has changed my life, because I realized that was all I'd been doing. And God is using this truth to untangle me.

When we strive, we're trying to be something we're not or get something we don't have. It's a constant state of discontent, feeding the belief there is always something better just beyond our reach. All we need to do is work harder. So we do. We buy into the great lie that says we're in control of our lives—the lie that whispers it's up to us to earn acceptance and approval.

But God tells us to know that *he* is God. He reminds us to stop asking others for validation because that was never his plan. So why do we spend so much time and effort trying to convince the world we're worthy of love? Why can't we rest knowing that God fully approves of us?

Even when you mess up, he sees who you are instead of what you've done. Those seasons where you made bad choice after bad choice mixed with bad choice (yeah, that one) didn't scare him off. His perfect love for you never wavered. And even better, there is nothing you can do, more or less, to alter that truth in any way.

Sometimes I struggle to wrap my mind around God's unconditional love because we live in a conditional world. That's why he tells us to *know* him. Because when we do, he starts to show us the way he sees us. We start seeing who we really are.

The Hebrew word for *know* is *yada*, which means to be well-known, to be recognized—like a familiar friend, someone you're well-acquainted with. It's not distant knowledge of a person, but rather an intimate and personal one.

It's your best friend who knows your goofy internal dialogue by the expression on your face, making you both fall into unstoppable laughter. It's your husband who knows your high-maintenance, slightly OCD drink order at Starbucks, and can get it for you without fail. It's your mom who can recall every detail of your high school career . . . the good, the bad, and the ugly. As women, don't we so desperately want to be *known* like that? So does God.

He created us for community. He loves to reveal himself in nature, through a song on the radio, or by those consistent and persistent messages that flash before us. God's story is the Bible, and somehow he makes it alive and relevant every day.

Can you think of a time when a Scripture jumped off the page and spoke directly into your situation? God longs to connect with us in prayer and delights when we take the time to discuss life with him. Every time we open our Bible, sit through a sermon, praise and worship to music, or attend a Bible study, it shows God we want to know him more intimately.

Jeremiah 29:13 says, "When you search for me, yes, search for me with all your heart, you will find me" (CEB). God wants us to search for him wholeheartedly so he can reveal who he is . . . and who we are.

~~~

After a short temper tantrum at the thought of giving up my online presence for a month, I was overcome by the realization that my heavenly Father wanted to spend time with me. Me. With all the busyness of the world and the cries for his intervention, God wanted one-on-one time to connect with *me*. Tears flooded my eyes as I whispered "Yes."

July 2012 was a sweet month. Rather than spend time calculating my worth through social media numbers, I connected to the heart of God. I was deeply aware of his presence in my life. We had daylong conversations about whatever popped into my head, even the crazy stuff. I saw him all over my life.

During that time, he revealed lies buried under negative thoughts and behaviors. He gave me spiritual eyes and ears to know the truth. He blessed me with revelation and healing. I began to recognize how desperate I'd been for love, trying anything to be seen and validated. I saw my striving and how it was damaging my self-esteem. I started seeing all my tangles, and that changed me. It was the beginning of the end—the end of allowing the world to tangle my self-worth.

In Mark 5, we meet a woman desperate for healing. She'd been living with a condition that caused her to bleed, and chronic blood loss probably meant anemia and physical weakness. For twelve years, she had sought medical help so she'd be considered "acceptable" in her community.

Bleeding made her unclean and therefore unwelcomed. Going

out in public was humiliating because she faced judgment and ridicule. Can't you just imagine how she struggled with feelings of rejection, abandonment, fear, and loneliness? Her ailment defined her, making her feel worthless and unlovable. Those twelve years had robbed so much from her.

She tried everything she knew to be healed. She'd subjected herself to barbaric tests and remedies, spending all her money searching for a cure. But instead of helping, Scripture tells us, the treatments made her worse. She was hopeless. And then she heard Jesus was near.

With great expectations, this frail woman slipped on her sandals and walked thirty miles to find the Healer.[1] She was at the end of her rope, and decided it was time for Jesus. Where the world had failed her, she hoped he could help. *If I just touch his clothes, I will be healed*, she thought (see Mark 5:28 NIV).

She wrestled her way through the crowd, reached out her hand, and touched the edge of his cloak. Verse 29 tells us "Immediately her bleeding stopped and she felt in her body that she was freed from her suffering" (NIV).

She had tried everything within her own strength to handle her struggle. She'd put her faith in worldly solutions to heal her condition. She'd spent her money on remedies. She'd spent her time on doctors. And she'd spent her hope on miracles. All she knew to do was to try and heal her condition with the resources she had. She was living in her *giftedness*.

But with no success, she decided to try something new. She went to find Jesus. In her heart, she knew it was time to live in her *godliness*. Her abilities had failed her. And when she stopped relying on herself and reached out to him, he healed her. And it changed everything.

This woman was no longer the town outcast. She could be out and about without feeling ashamed. Instead of being rejected, she was now an accepted part of her community. Jesus had redeemed her reputation, removed her shame, restored her confidence, and rebuilt her sense of worth. Because of him, she was free.

When we *cease striving* in our giftedness and relying on our own strength and ability to find self-worth, we will be changed too. Knowing God is the only way to truly know ourselves, because we begin to see who we really are through his eyes.

But this isn't what the Enemy wants for us. He doesn't want us to know we're fully loved, fully known, and fully accepted by our heavenly Father. That kind of knowledge is dangerous to Satan. How will he keep us striving to be *good enough* if we know we already are? His plan from the beginning was to have us working for approval and feeling like a failure. And he lies to make that happen.

"He couldn't stand the truth because there wasn't a shred of truth in him. When the Liar speaks, he makes it up out of his lying nature and fills the world with lies" (John 8:45). The Enemy makes up lies and then spreads them. Nothing he says is based in truth. Not one thing. Do you recognize his language? Here are common phrases the Enemy likes to whisper to us:

You can't . . .

You won't . . .

You'll never be . . .

You'll always be . . .

You shouldn't have . . .

You should have . . .

Even typing these out, I can feel the guilt and shame attached to each one. I'm reminded of times they've caused me to feel rejected. My wound of worthlessness gets poked by these phrases. Where have you heard them lately? In your marriage? As a mom? As a friend? In your work? As a daughter?

When we allow these *not good enough* messages to sink into our DNA, we'll strive to prove them wrong. We'll outspend our budget to keep up with the Joneses. We'll sacrifice our morals and standards just to fit in. We'll change how we act and how we look, hoping someone will see our worth. We'll let our value as a woman be determined by how well we perform. And we will become a tangled mess.

We are a tangled mess.

We need a divine untangling by the only One with the ability to untie our *not good enough* from the people and places we've tied it to in the world. Only God can straighten out the knots that keep us feeling worthless.

The current psychological trend is that we can do it ourselves. Apparently, the power to be enlightened and change ourselves is found within. Truth is, I don't know where. We don't always know why we do what we do. Right? We may not even know we're doing it, for Pete's sake. So just how are we supposed to find the answers hidden inside and fix our own brokenness?

There are times I'll react defensively to my husband's suggestion, but I don't know why. I'll feel ashamed over my response to a situation without any good reason. Something innocuous will trigger me and I can't make sense of it. So how am I expected to heal myself?

We're not. We can't. That's just a bunch of bunk. Listen, I've tried. I've spent countless hours and money at counseling offices hoping for someone to fix me. I've stared in the mirror and said sweet things to myself. I've visualized the "new me." I've read the books and listened to the self-help CDs. I've structured my day to have self-care. I've tried journaling my deepest thoughts. And here I am—still struggling to feel *good enough*.

While those in the mental health field serve a valuable role, only Jesus can change a heart. All those self-help ideas are thought up by well-intentioned people, but we need healing, not behavior modification. We need a touch from Jesus to untangle our messy, black and blue hearts and find lasting value. No earthly doctor or remedy can do that.

It really is all about Jesus. He is the answer. He is the only One who can unknot the Enemy's lies that strangle our self-worth, and remind us of the truth of who we are. With him, we win. "They defeated him by the blood of the Lamb and by their testimony" (Rev. 12:11 TLB).

We are the "they" in this verse, and the Enemy is "him." Jesus is how we overcome the *not good enough* knots that Satan has strategically created in our lives. And hearing the untangled victories of others helps to strengthen our weary bones through the process.

Because of Jesus, it's possible to find victory in the battle for your self-worth.

～ ⚬ ～

Some may think it sounds too "simple," asking Jesus to untangle our worth from the world. Some might find it too "charismatic" because they don't believe miracles still happen. Many don't think the Bible is relevant today as our handbook for living an abundant life. Still others may not believe a personal relationship is possible with a "faraway" God. But what have you got to lose? Since you picked up this book, or someone you love has passed it on to you, chances are the other things you've tried haven't worked.

In the Bible, there are thirty-seven miracles attributed to Jesus. From restoring sight to healing an ear, from withering a blooming tree to blooming a withering hand, from turning water into wine to casting out demons, he changed things. And he transformed not only the lives of those he healed but also the lives of those who witnessed his miracles and heard about them. As a matter of fact, we're still encouraged by the things Jesus did while on earth.

But let's think about here and now. Can you remember a time in your life where God showed up big? Or think of when you saw his supernatural power intersect the life of another? Maybe you didn't realize it was him, but there was no other explanation for it. It seemed miraculous.

The disease disappeared.

The marriage found healing.

The money anonymously appeared.

The hardened heart softened.

The prodigal came home.

The career doors opened.

The broken relationship was restored.

Let's get even more personal. Have you been knocked to your knees by a hurtful comment and felt an unexplainable peace after you cried out to God? Can you think back to a time when something that should have triggered those familiar feelings of rejection didn't? Do you remember the day you looked into a mirror and actually liked what you saw—even though it wasn't perfect? Can you recall the day you didn't crave the approval of another? It seemed miraculous, didn't it? Take a minute right now to thank God. That was the work of the divine detangler.

God still performs miracles today. He is alive and active, and wants to untangle you from the knots of insecurity that are choking your self-worth. You may never see Jesus this side of heaven but you will most certainly see his handiwork. You might not feel the untangling process but you will see the results. No matter what anyone says, the touch of Jesus is the most powerful force we will ever experience and it's available here and now. For me and for you.

Why is Jesus so willing to help us? It's because he is eternally invested in us. When you were created, it was with great intention. He thought through every detail of your life and made you different from everyone else. And while the world may tell you differently, that's a good thing. He knew what strengths you'd have as well as the challenges you'd face. From how you look to the interests you hold to the experiences you'd have, God approved them all right from the beginning. And all through Scripture, he confirms just how valuable you are to him.

You are a unique creation.

> You alone created my inner being.
>> You knitted me together inside my mother.
> I will give thanks to you
>> because I have been so amazingly and miraculously made.
>> Your works are miraculous, and my soul is fully aware of this. (Ps. 139:13–16 GW)

You are the apple of his eye.

> Protect me as you would your very eyes;
>> hide me in the shadow of your wings. (Ps. 17:8 GNT)

He knows you completely.

And the very hairs of your head are all numbered. (Matt. 10:30 TLB)

You are accepted by God.

But you are the ones chosen by God, chosen for the high calling of priestly work, chosen to be a holy people, God's instruments to do his work and speak out for him, to tell others of the night-and-day difference he made for you—from nothing to something, from rejected to accepted. (1 Pet. 2:9–10)

What you need matters.

And with all his abundant wealth through Christ Jesus, my God will supply all your needs. (Phil. 4:19 GNT)

You belong.

But now you belong to Christ Jesus, and though you once were far away from God, now you have been brought very near to him because of what Jesus Christ has done for you with his blood. (Eph. 2:13 TLB)

You have a future.

I have it all planned out—plans to take care of you, not abandon you, plans to give you the future you hope for. (Jer. 29:11 Message)

In God's eyes, you are perfect.

So God created human beings, making them to be like himself. (Gen. 1:27 GNT)

These verses helped untangle the little four-year-old heart in me that was told *you're worth nothing*. The more I read Scriptures like these, the more I believe who God says I am. His Word carries healing power, and Psalm 107:20 confirms it: "He sends forth his word and heals them and rescues them from the pit and destruction" (AMP).

But there's one Scripture from the Bible that stands alone. It reveals the price God paid to combat the *not good enough* messages we'd hear from the world.

For God so greatly loved and dearly prized the world that He [even] gave up His only begotten (unique) Son, so that whoever believes in (trusts in, clings to, relies on) him shall not perish (come to destruction, be lost) but have eternal (everlasting) life. For God did not send the Son into the world in order to judge (to reject, to condemn, to pass sentence on) the world, but that the world might find salvation and be made safe and sound through him. (John 3:16–17 AMP)

The way this translation reads moves me to tears. Maybe it's because I'm humbled God loves me so. Maybe it's because he offers me safety in a world that's careless with my heart. Maybe it's because this passage speaks to the wounded part in me that says *you're worth nothing* and reminds me I'm worth *everything*.

So knowing that I matter so much, sometimes I wonder why God has allowed my self-worth to become such a tangled mess. Why didn't he protect me from the abuse? The bad choices? The crooked path? Why didn't he intervene earlier rather than let me become so knotted up in an overwhelming sense of worthlessness? Maybe you've wondered the same for your life too.

> I have told you this so that you will have peace by being united to me. The world will make you suffer. But be brave! I have defeated the world! (John 16:33 GNT)

Unfortunately, suffering is inevitable. There's no way to escape it. In this life we will encounter rude comments, deep heart bruises, mean girls, affliction, betrayal, ridicule, manipulation, hate, and the like. To think differently is unrealistic.

God never promised us exemption from pain. It's part of living on Planet Earth. But he does promise transformation and deliverance if we hold on to him through it. When we trust God, we suffer through the hard times with the hope of restoration. And we know that if he allows the tangle it's only because he will use it for our benefit and his glory. He uses those tangles to accomplish something in us. And in a way only he understands, there's great purpose in them.

⌐◦୧◦⌐

God has been untangling the mother of all knots in my life. But I'll be honest, it feels terribly vulnerable to share this with you because it's a deep wound—maybe the deepest. When God asked me to include it in this book, it freaked my beak. Exposing it felt unsafe, and I didn't see any good reason to publicly disclose the hardest struggle in my life to people I don't even know.

But walking out of bondage and into freedom requires bringing our struggles into the light. Anything kept in the dark—kept secret—is fair game for the Enemy. He pokes our black and blue heart with them, reinforcing their messages of fear, shame, guilt, and worthlessness.

Through this untangling season, I've learned to trust God with those painful places. Now when I share my story with groups of women or my book and blog audience, it's another layer of healing for me. After lots of prayer and encouragement from friends, I knew this story must be in this book. And you know what I think? I'm certain many of you will be able to relate. Let me back up a bit.

My weight has always been a place of deep wounding. As much as I've tried to and wanted to, I have never been able to meet the world's standard of thin. I've bought into every diet gimmick and eating fad. I've signed up with local gyms. I've tried the latest exercise crazes—the ones that promised fast results. Right. I've drunk the shakes, walked the miles, and counted the calories, but any positive results were always short-lived.

One time, I actually prayed this: "God, will you please let me wake up tomorrow thin? I know sometimes we have to do the work, but other times you do it. Remember parting the Red Sea? The Jordan River? You just did it to bless the Israelites. Won't you bless me with losing weight overnight?" Yep. Honest truth. I'm sure he got a good laugh from that one. And when I woke up the next morning the same, I felt a big "request denied" stamp hit my already bruised heart.

Growing up, I was constantly reminded that thin was in, which obviously meant I wasn't. I was told I should be skinny like all my other friends. By the way, *should* is such a shaming word. Don't use it on the people you love.

Instead I was the athlete, more concerned with muscle strength than skinny jeans. I played soccer, softball, and tennis, and was great at them all. But because I wasn't rail thin, I never felt beautiful—never felt lovable. Hurtful comments would trigger a replay of my abuser's voice in my mind—*A real woman is thin. So if you're not, you're worthless.*

When my abuser showed me pornographic magazines, telling me "real" women looked like they did, I believed him. I had lost my innocence that day. When I was held in the apartment while he spoke these lies, my little four-year-old self-worth made an unconscious agreement—I had to look like the women on the pages of that magazine to matter.

Fast-forward to present day. My good friend introduced me to a pastor who guided people into an encounter with Jesus that's life-changing. I'd seen this ministry in action. I'd watched people experience freedom from the lies that had kept them in bondage. And while their tangles may have been different, the remedy was the same—they asked Jesus to untangle them.

I made a day-long appointment because I figured it would take that long. Let's just say I've lived a lot of life. I wasn't in crisis, but this ministry time was the next step in my journey. I knew it.

In the weeks before my session, all of my defenses were already kicking in and I didn't even realize it. Based on what I'd seen with others, I tried to plot out how my appointment might look. I spent time thinking through what God most likely wanted to deal with. I made lists and jotted down notes to share, certain all my prep would be helpful. I was striving to look all-together and organized, certain it would earn me points somehow. I wasn't exactly excited to go, but I was ready.

That day, God revealed places where I'd been listening to messages of worthlessness for years. We worked through guilt. We uncovered shame. And we dealt with other tangles that had kept me knotted up. The work was hard and exhausting. There were lots of tears and snot, but it was freeing to unearth some root causes of my *not good enough* feelings.

You know how good you feel after stepping out of a hot shower, the effects of the day washed away? You smell shampoo and body wash lingering in the air. And as you slip on yummy pjs and crawl into bed, you feel safe, secure, and clean. That's how I felt that afternoon. We had done some major work, it was early evening, and I was ready to call it a day. Then the pastor asked me another question.

"Carey, this isn't something I normally ask, but God has brought it to mind several times today. I just can't let you leave without addressing it."

I'd willingly made the appointment, looking for God to connect some dots. I wanted divine intervention. I knew I needed healing. So if God had more in store, my thought was . . . *bring it*. Then he looked me straight in the eyes and asked, "How much did you weigh in college?"

And there it was. The topic others had used as a weapon against me, the one I'd used against myself, had surfaced again. While I was hemorrhaging on the inside, I remained calm on the outside. I'd learned that trick long ago—never let them see they've hurt you. I looked up at my betrayer and said, "What? I don't know. I guess I gained the freshman fifteen like most others."

In an instant, it seemed all the healing work we'd spent the day sorting through was undone. Gone. I was furious at the pastor and incensed at God, and all I wanted to do was run and hide. Weight wasn't something I discussed even with my husband, much less a man I barely knew. It felt calculated, cruel, and hateful, and I can't remember the last time I was so angry.

"Until you untangle your self-esteem from your weight, you'll never feel good enough," he continued.

I'm sure he said a million other things, but after these words I stopped listening. I was done. I collected my things, faked pleasantries, walked out of the building, and closed the car door behind me. As I drove from the parking lot, I yelled, "God, what in the heck was *that*?" Honestly, my choice of words was a bit edgier—and there were lots of them. It wasn't my finest moment. How did I not see this coming? How had my defenses failed me? I was so mad I could spit.

My family greeted me at the door, excited to hear all of what God had revealed. I had no intention of sharing a thing, of course. I quickly excused myself, climbed into bed, pulled the covers over my broken heart, and went to sleep. I hated everyone and wanted to be left alone.

I woke the next morning feeling worse than the day before. My *not good enough* tangle was knotted tighter than ever. Sleep hadn't helped a thing and I was too tired to fight. Little did I know God was about to loosen that knot in a miraculous way.

While everyone else was still sleeping, I grabbed coffee, curled up in my chair, and watched the sunrise. My husband walked into the room and said, "Are you okay? Are we okay? You barely talked to me last night."

With all of my defenses in shambles, I opened up and shared the previous day's events. My sweet husband listened to me sob through my story, and something in him shifted. He became angry on my behalf, ready to pick up the phone and let the pastor have it. My man was ready to fight for me. He wanted to protect me. And in that moment—maybe for the first time—I felt *worth the effort*. The knot loosened a bit.

I convinced him not to call because I knew the pastor was doing what God had asked. But because I was inconsolable and he felt helpless, Wayne sent for reinforcements. He knows his limits. So often, our men just don't know what to do when we're a mess.

Wayne will sometimes suggest I phone a friend when I'm upset, especially when we've been talking about my frustration for more than five minutes. Men are fixers and women just like to chew on things for a while. But that day he was tender and strong, and it spoke huge healing things into my heart. And an hour later, there was a knock on my door.

My friend hugged me and listened while I shared the experience again. Rather than see it as an attack, she saw God all over it. "Carcy, this was a divine set-up. God knew it was the only way to catch you with your defenses down." Her words resonated. She was spot-on.

Abuse victims develop an intricate set of ramparts to protect themselves from being hurt again. Some we're aware of. Others, not so much. We adopt the posture of self-protection because we're sure no one else will protect us. After all, they haven't in the past. And honestly, some of my defenses are weird.

For example, when I close the slatted window blinds in my home, they have to face down so people can't see up into the house. When I go into a restaurant or coffeehouse, I scope out all the exits and know the quickest way to each of them. I always case the place for potential predators and watch for any signs of danger. At the theatre I choose aisle seats so I can get out faster if something bad happens. And more often than not, I'm the driver because I feel safer when I'm behind the wheel. It's always been me against the world. I wonder, what are some ways you protect yourself?

The bottom line is that I know how to take care of myself. Since my abuse, I've put on my armor and stood guard over my own heart. I've been the only one I could trust. But in all my years of self-preservation, I hadn't developed an escape route for a situation like this.

The Great Physician had lanced a deep wound with perfect precision—a wound more diseased than I'd realized—and I couldn't respond quick enough to stop the bleeding. The tangle had been well-guarded for years. And God exposed it so he could heal it.

At the core of the wound were my abuser's words telling me I was worthless. I'd made an agreement that my worth as a woman was dependent on looking just like the images on the pages of that pornographic magazine. The result was a covenant that said my worth was determined by my weight. This revelation was huge!

As my friend and I prayed for God to break that agreement, he showed me a picture in my mind's eye of a heart. It seemed nice and pink and healthy. Then a knife appeared and began cutting off pieces of it here and there. It wasn't bloody or gross. And as I looked closer, I could see that the portions the knife removed were discolored—diseased. This was a visual representation of what God was doing to my heart.

We read about circumcision in the Bible. For the Israelite men, it was a religious rite and symbolized the covenant solidarity for the descendants of Abraham (see Gen. 17:10). But it wasn't only a physical mark; there was—and is—a spiritual interpretation. "So circumcise the foreskin of your [minds and] hearts; be no longer stubborn and hardened" (Deut. 10:16 AMP).

That day, God circumcised my heart. He canceled the old covenant I'd made with myself—the one that said my weight determined my worth. He cut away the parts of me that kept me striving for acceptance and approval. He cut off areas that left me feeling like I'd never be good enough. Gone are the parts that told me I was a failure for not being a size 6. He removed the sections that made me feel inferior to the images of women in the media. God cut away the lies of worthlessness. Because I was so tangled up in these beliefs, amputating them was something only he could do.

Proverbs 4:23 says, "Guard your heart more than anything else, because the source of your life flows from it" (GW). Those are strong words—*more than anything*. God is saying that protecting our hearts should be our biggest priority. Why? Because all of our emotions, thoughts, and actions originate there.

I also love the Good News translation of the same verse: "Be careful how you think; your life is shaped by your thoughts." Haven't you seen this play out in your own circumstances? I sure have in mine. Because I've lived my life feeling inferior and unworthy, most of my choices and decisions have reflected that belief. It's become my truth. My modus operandi.

As we prayed, I immediately felt an oppression lift from me. But I didn't see confirmation of God's divine untangling until Wayne brought home cake a few days later. And not just any cake, but an oversized piece of red velvet cake topped with gobs of cream cheese icing—easily one of my all-time favorites. Sweet mother.

When my thoughtful husband proudly walked in the door and handed me this little slice of heaven, he was beaming. But not me. I said, "Why in the world did you buy me *this*?" Honestly, I was a little perturbed. He rarely brings home foodie gifts because he knows it's tricky for me. Eating them would pile on guilt and shame, reminders of hurtful comments I'd heard about food choices growing up. This oversized piece of cake poked that fresh wound.

But this time was different. As the exclamation escaped my mouth, it didn't feel right anymore. I looked at Wayne and said, "Wow. I'm sorry about that. Thank you for the gift. It's perfect." And girls, I ate the whole stinkin' thing. All of it. And I loved every minute of it. No guilt. No worry. No condemnation. No taunting blasts from the past. Something in me had shifted.

The Holy Spirit gently whispered, *Beloved, your weight doesn't determine your worth. You're stunning to the One who made you.* And you know what? I'm beginning to believe it. I'm on the path of untangling the wounded parts of me. But it's a journey.

Think about it for a minute. Where are you desperate to measure up to others? What are you doing to try to prove your worth? In what roles have you been striving for approval? Where are you trying to overcome those *not good enough* messages? Is it:

In all things surrounding being a woman?

In your role as a godly wife?

By being a supermom?

As a domestic goddess?

In being a good friend?

To your online community?

In your work?

I know there are many reasons you're tangled. Some are because of the things people have said or the ways they've treated you. Others are societal. The world is quick to tell you who you should be and remind you of who you are not. It's also the Enemy. He looks for ways to bring to mind those times you've failed. And other times it's you. You bully yourself with words and thoughts, and refuse to extend grace to yourself when you mess up.

I know you've tried to loosen the knots yourself. Some ways have been unhealthy responses to your insecurities, like overconsuming alcohol, using prescription or street drugs, and filling that emptiness with food. You may have coped through retail therapy. There is a high you experience from finding that perfect shirt or sheet set. But in reality, spending money is merely a distraction from the things that knot you up.

Maybe you've withdrawn from community, building walls to protect your heart from another *not good enough* reminder. Have you created a better version of yourself online? Maybe you've tried to earn acceptance by becoming a perfectionist and overachiever, looking for recognition in one area so others won't notice where you fall short in another.

Think about it. How have you tried to untangle your self-esteem? Chances are, any success you've had has been a short-term fix. Truth is, we can't untangle ourselves. Maybe it's time to stop trying.

Listen to the Word of God as he encourages his people, promising restoration after their terrible suffering.

> I will give you back your health again and heal your wounds. Now you are called "The Outcast" and "Jerusalem, the Place Nobody Wants." But, says the Lord, when I bring you home again from your captivity and restore your fortunes, Jerusalem will be rebuilt upon her ruins; the palace will be reconstructed as it was before. (Jer. 30:17–18 TLB)

I love this guarantee. We need the Lord, don't we? Life has left us heartsick and wounded. We've felt unwanted, like outcasts. Those *not good enough* messages have kept us bound up in worthlessness. In our shame, we've been unable to believe God could love us and accept us as we are. We've tried to rebuild our self-worth in all the wrong ways. We've spent years striving to restore our broken hearts on our own. And that's why we're still tangled. All of our efforts have left us more insecure than ever.

The only way—*the only way*—we can be free is to let God untangle us. Our best efforts have fallen short time and time again because we are limited by our human condition. But he has God-sized abilities we'll never fully understand this side of heaven.

And while he is able to miraculously heal us in an instant, chances are he won't. We didn't get this tangled overnight, right? There is a lot of learning along the way that's key to our healing journey. So grab your water bottle and lace up your shoes, sweet friend.

As God loosens each knot of insecurity, you'll experience the freedom it brings—maybe for the first time. He will highlight circumstances that have triggered feelings of worthlessness and remove their power over your life. You'll learn to embrace your beauty as a woman through the eyes of God rather than the scales of the world. He will help you distinguish the Enemy's lies from the truth of who you really are. And in a way only God can do, he will take your black and blue heart and make it new.

So what are you waiting for? Go ahead . . . ask him. Ask him right now. Ask God to untangle your self-worth from those unhealthy places. Ask him to silence those *not good enough* voices. Ask him to anchor your sense of value to Jesus, the One who gave his life to show the value of yours.

Ask him, because you are worth it.

Lord, I am ready for the journey to freedom. Lead the way!
Thank you that you've already cleared the path for me, and

that you won't leave me knotted up in my insecurities. Thank you for loving me in the middle of my tangles, the places where I've felt so unlovable. I want to know I am good enough!

Would you please give me the ears and eyes to know you are with me? Would you guide me through the tangle so I don't get tripped up along the way? I need resolve to stick with it, especially when it gets hard. Please encourage me at just the right time. Give me hope that freedom is possible.

I'm tired of living in defeat, afraid I'll never measure up. Rewire my self-esteem so I'm confident in who I am because of Jesus. Help me off the performance-based treadmill that's wearing me out. Silence my tongue when I start to speak lies to myself. Remind me to seek no one's approval but yours, and to cry out to you when I am feeling weak and weary.

Dress me in your mighty spiritual armor so I'm protected against the Enemy's arrows, and go before me so I can follow your lead. I understand now that you are my defender and shield.

I don't want to live a safe and guarded life anymore. I want to live the adventure you have called me to live. I want to love with a pure heart, and receive love with confidence. Give me your courage and strength in those dark hours when I feel scared and weak. I need perseverance, perspective, and passion in every battle that comes my way.

Help me to cease striving and know you are God. My God. My Creator and Restorer. I love you, Lord. Thank you for loving me first.

In the powerful name of Jesus. Amen.

Epilogue

When I married Carey, I had no idea how deep her wounds were or how tough her scar tissue was. She had spent a lifetime fortifying herself against anyone and everyone, fearful of letting anyone get too close. Because if they got too close, they might hurt her. Or worse, they might see her the way she saw herself: devoid of value. Unlovable. Worthless.

Back in those early days immediately after we got married, we were both incredibly fragile. To her, any perceived slight from me, no matter how minor, meant I didn't love her. And for me, any action she took outside my narrowly defined marital expectations was an indication that she was trying to control me.

Seven years into our marriage, I had little more understanding of her than I did on our wedding day. Carey used to jokingly tell me, "Don't act like you know me." The sad truth was that for a long time all I could do was act, because I *didn't* know her. That had as much to do with my failures as a husband—my own tangled self-worth issues—as it did with her emotional defenses. But I won't be delving into my issues here; the only book about untangling I feel qualified to write would be for inept fly fishermen who struggle with keeping their line from fouling in the trees. And my guess is that you don't fall in that target audience.

Now, fifteen years after we said our vows, I know my wife. Let me be clear: I don't claim to always understand her, and any man who makes that statement about his wife is either a fool or a liar. But I do *know* her. I know that when I come home from work and surprise her with a Caramel Light Frappuccino, it puts a smile on her face that makes the overpriced coffee worth every penny. I know that when she wants to talk about some challenge she's facing she isn't looking for me to solve it; she just wants to share her heart with me. And I know that when I leave a note on the kitchen counter telling her I love her, she finally believes me.

The first time Carey finally mustered up the courage to tell me the details of her abuse was more than a dozen years after we were married. I wept. I wept for the little girl she'd been and the innocence she'd lost. For the woman she would have been if not for that monster. I wept for the damage his actions had done to our marriage.

And I wept because there wasn't a single thing I could do about it.

But as Carey has gone through her untangling, I've rejoiced. Because I don't see a helpless, frightened little girl anymore. Nor do I see the saggy, wrinkled, eyebrow-impaired woman she claims to be earlier in this book. I've gone through some untangling of my own, and it's allowed me to see her the way God does. And what's even better, it's the way I think she's starting to see herself too:

The warrior stands in a sea of gold. Waves of tall, dry grass roll in the breeze. It's peaceful, but most fields look that way before battle.

Her armor is simple: unadorned, brushed gray metal. She wears a heavy breastplate from neck to waist, and below it a leather skirt that ends just above her knees. Her shins are sheathed in metal greaves. Her strong arms are bare, save for a metal bracer on each wrist. Her hands grip the hilt of a giant, two-handed sword, point resting on the ground. By the easy way she carries the weapon, it's obvious she knows it well. She scans the horizon, her blue-green eyes filled with a steely resolve. Her blonde hair is wild and bright against the gray of the gathering clouds. A storm is brewing. And the warrior is ready to battle for her God.

Wayne

Notes

Chapter 2 The First Tangle

1. Matthew Gilbert, "Self-Help Books and the Promise of Change," *Boston Globe,* January 14, 2014, http://www.bostonglobe.com/arts/books/2014/01/14/self-help-books-and-promise-change/4nJqRBpinOSWQ4wU536jPP/story.html.

Chapter 3 The Tangled Expectations of Women

1. Carl Jung, *The Red Book: Liber Novus*, facsimile ed., Sonu Shamdasani, ed. (New York: W. W. Norton, 2009).

2. Jean Kilborne, "Beauty ... and the Beast of Advertising," Center for Media Literary, accessed October 14, 2014, http://www.medialit.org/reading-room/beautyand-beast-advertising.

3. Marianne Mychaskiw, "Report: Women Spend an Average of $15,000 on Makeup in Their Lifetimes," *InStyle*, April 17, 2013, http://news.instyle.com/2013/04/17/women-makeup-spending-facts.

4. "11 Facts About Body Image," DoSomething.org, accessed October 14, 2014, http://www.dosomething.org/tipsandtools/11-facts-about-body-image.

5. "Eating Disorders Statistics," ANAD, accessed October 14, 2014, http://www.anad.org/get-information/about-eating-disorders/eating-disorders-statistics/.

6. Amy Odell, "Women Over 50 Plagued By Eating Disorders, Body-Image Issues," *Buzzfeed*, accessed November 25, 2014, http://www.buzzfeed.com/amyodell/many-women-over-age-50-struggle-with-eating-disord.

7. Ethan A. Huff, "The United States of Plastic Surgery: Americans Spent $11 Billion Last Year on Face Lifts, Botox, Breast Augmentations," *Natural News*, May 2, 2013, http://www.naturalnews.com/040164_plastic_surgery_breast_augmentation_botox.html.

8. Lauren Bacall, as quoted in *The Daily Telegraph*, March 2, 1988.

9. Geoff Williams, "The Heavy Price of Losing Weight," *U.S. News and World Report*, January 2, 2013, http://money.usnews.com/money/personal-finance/articles/2013/01/02/the-heavy-price-of-losing-weight.

10. Paul Suggett, "Sex In Advertising," About.com, accessed October 14, 2014, http://advertising.about.com/od/advertisingprojects/a/Sex-In-Advertising.htm.

Chapter 4 It Takes Two to Tangle

1. As quoted in Robert Byrne, ed., *The 2,548 Best Things Anybody Ever Said*, repr. ed. (New York: Simon and Schuster, 2003), #149.

2. Boze Hadleigh, *Holy Matrimony! Better Halves and Bitter Halves: Actors, Athletes, Comedians, Directors, Divas, Philosophers, Poets, Politicians, and Other Celebs Talk about Marriage* (Kansas City, MO: Andrews McMeel Publishing, 2012).

3. As quoted in Joan and Lew Koch, "The Surest Way to Be Alone Is to Get Married," *The Southeast Missourian*, October 30, 1974, 6.

Chapter 5 Tangled Up in Our Kids

1. Dillon Burroughs, "1 Samuel 8: The Problem with Comparisons," *Holy Writ*, December 5, 2012, http://www.patheos.com/blogs/holywrit/2012/12/1-samuel-8-the-problem-with-comparisons/.

Chapter 6 Tangled in Domestic Disappointment

1. Joyce Meyer, "Enjoy Your Whole Day," *Starting Your Day Right: Devotions for Each Morning of the Year*, (New York: Warner Faith, 2003) 307.

Chapter 7 Friendship: Tried, True, or Tangled?

1. Dietrich Bonhoeffer, *Life Together: The Classic Exploration of Faith in Community*, (New York: Harper & Row, 1954), 20.

2. As quoted in Zachary Stieber, "Friendship Day 2014: 21 Quotes, Messages, Sayings for a Happy Friendship Day (and Date)," *Epoch Times*, August 1, 2014, http://m.theepochtimes.com/n3/833739-friendship-day-21-quotes-messages-and-sayings-for-friends-date/?sidebar=hotarticle.

3. "Toba Beta, *Master of Stupidity* quotes," https://www.goodreads.com/quotes/362857-friendship-s-enemy-is-betrayal.

Chapter 8 The Tangled Web of Social Media

1. Andrew Hough, "Why Women Constantly Lie about Life on Facebook," *The Telegraph*, March 12, 2013, http://www.telegraph.co.uk/technology/facebook/9925072/Why-women-constantly-lie-about-life-on-Facebook.html.

2. Ibid.

Chapter 10 The Divine Untangling

1. Liz Curtis Higgs, "The Woman Who Touched Jesus," *Today's Christian Woman*, January 2007, http://www.todayschristianwoman.com/articles/2007/january/woman-who-touched-jesus.html.

Carey Scott is an author, speaker, and certified Bible life coach who challenges women to be real—not perfect—even when real is messy. She speaks and writes to women about the everyday issues that matter most to their hearts, always weaving in powerful reminders of their immeasurable value. Her desire is to help women overcome the not-good-enough messages that keep them from loving who God created them to be. She was born and raised in Texas, but dropped her Southern twang when she moved to Colorado, where she now lives with her husband, their two kids, and an array of furry critters. While Carey is very much a homebody, you'll often find her hunkered down in the corner of a coffee shop, trying to string together a well-crafted sentence. If you see her, head over and say hello.

You can also find her here:
Website and blog: www.CareyScottTalks.com
Facebook: https://www.faccbook.com/careyscotttalks
Twitter: https://twitter.com/careyscotttalks
Pinterest: http://www.pinterest.com/careyscotttalks/
Instagram: http://instagram.com/careyscotttalks

For exclusive podcasts, printables, and other freebies related to *Untangled*, please visit www.TheUntangledBook.com.

Get to know

 at

www.CareyScottTalks.com

- Find free audio and downloadable resources
- Read the blog and sign up for the newsletter
- Book Carey to speak to your group